Raising Upright Kids in an
Upside-Down World

D0104314

Dr. Ray Guarendi

Raising Upright Kids
in an
Upside-Down World

EWTN PUBLISHING, INC.
Irondale, Alabama

EWTN Publishing, Inc.
5817 Old Leeds Road, Irondale, AL 35210

Distributed by Sophia Institute Press, Box 5284, Manchester, NH 03108.

Library of Congress Cataloging-in-Publication Data

Names: Guarendi, Ray, author.
Title: Raising upright kids in an upside-down world / Dr. Ray Guarendi.
Description: Irondale, Alabama : EWTN Publishing, Inc., 2020. | Includes
    bibliographical references. | Summary: "How to raise morally upright
    children in today's culture"— Provided by publisher.
Identifiers: LCCN 2019047908 | ISBN 9781682781050 (paperback) | ISBN
    9781682781067 (ebook)
Subjects: LCSH: Child rearing—Religious aspects—Christianity. |
    Parenting—Religious aspects—Christianity. | Christianity and culture.
Classification: LCC BV4529 .G84 2020 | DDC 248.8/45—dc23
LC record available at https://lccn.loc.gov/2019047908

To those parents who persevere heroically
through a culture that besieges them

Contents

1

The Anti-Parents

The year: 1880. The place: Springfield, Ohio. The year: 1662. The place: Genoa, Italy. The year: 122. The place: Alexandria, Egypt.

Times and places far distant from one another. So, too, their cultures. What do they all have in common? Historians might debate the answers, but one thing all could agree on: The family—or the clan or the tribe—was the undisputed teacher of the youth. For better or worse, they were the dominant shapers of the next generation. Consequently, what most children absorbed when young, they retained when old.

Those who opposed the guardian adults had little or no reach into the child's world. Their power to mold him into their image was minimal, if they had any at all.

Or so went the social reality for 99-plus percent of human history. The other fraction of 1 percent is happening today. In the last few generations of family life, at least in our culture, everything has changed.

Who Is This?

A sad but common scene in my office is that of parents struggling to fathom the wayward conduct of their teen or young adult. They feel helpless as he ignores or rejects the family's standards. Years of conscientious parenting are having waning influence. His moral trajectory looks to be veering from theirs at accelerating speed.

Hurting and confused, they ask, "Who is this? We didn't raise him this way!" And indeed, they didn't. These are good parents whose aim all along has been to instill solid character in their children. Along the way, however, they likely underestimated the power and persuasiveness of what opposed them—the surrounding culture. Not only does the culture talk and act differently from them, but it celebrates its way and belittles theirs.

As used here, the "culture" refers to society's reigning morals, attitudes, and conduct—in essence, what it values, what it pushes as acceptable and "enlightened" living.

One Child Too Many

Not only is the culture not fond of your way of raising children: It isn't all that fond of children themselves. Oh, kids are all right—in the proper, respectable number per household. You're generally permitted two before meeting society's judgment. If both are of the same sex, then three might be understandable: "You're trying for a girl, right?" Or, "You're hoping for a boy now, huh?"

Beyond three, though, the editorial comments multiply per child. You're being irresponsible, selfish (talk about irony), and soaking up more than your fair share of the rainforest.

Our society has wrapped its arms around a "liberating" carnal code: If it feels good—even if not—do it. Pretty much any sexual activity is applauded. Pretty much any, that is, except having one too many babies in marriage.

A reigning cultural commandment: Don't judge another's behavior—unless she's a married mother of more than two.

Upon visiting their physicians for a checkup for their third pregnancy, mothers are handed "family planning" brochures, as though they are afflicted with an illness that needs prevention.

A father of ten told me that after his fifth, he kept to himself news of his wife's pregnancies, as the congratulations were decreasing and the stunned silences increasing. Out-of-state relatives would just have to be shocked at his family's expansion at the next holiday.

There is risk in cornering veteran parents who've heard the same tiresome critiques and who are trained in fielding quirky queries from all the little people living around them.

"Is this all your family?" Of course not, our oldest is at home with the triplets.

"Are you thinking of getting fixed?" I didn't know I was broken.

"I'm glad it's you and not me." I think my kids are glad, too. (*Ouch!*)

This bent attitude toward the acceptable quota of children, at its very core, speaks to the collision between our society and traditional family life.

When my wife and I trooped through a public place with our ten adopted children, we got our share of stares, perhaps because of the sheepherding dog with us. Because our kids had a variety of skin colors, we weren't targets of the heavier critiques reserved for parents of ten biological kids. Adoption does lend a certain concession to family size.

Not always, though. A mother of eighteen special-needs adopted children said that with each child, she received more swipes than support. "What are you trying to prove?" was a familiar refrain. That she wanted to give a home to a child who needed one?

If you're accused of adding people to an already overpeopled world, ask a simple question: "How are you so sure you're not one of the too many?"

Raising Upright Kids in an Upside-Down World

Beyond Rebellion

"Adolescents rebel. It's a stage on their way to independence." So says the theory, held as developmental gospel. Reality says something different: Some kids rebel; some don't. Some a little, some a lot. Some for months, some for years.

No question, adolescence is a time of accelerating physical change. Bodies stretch; hormones surge; adult anatomy beckons. Yet rebellion for many teens remains time limited. It's a transient grab for multiplying freedoms and perks. Craving more independence than their parents know is good for them, they strain against the rules.

At peak rebellion, though, the teen still holds, however loosely, to what she has been taught. For a spell, she thinks herself more savvy and up to date than anybody over twenty-two. Life, however, in time compels a more grown-up (read: old person) outlook. To paraphrase Mark Twain: When I was eighteen, my father was the dumbest man in the world. I was amazed at how much smarter he got by the time I reached twenty-one.

Present-day teen rebellion seems more cultural than biological. Even the word "teenager" is fairly new to the child-rearing lexicon. Would a farm father in 1880 lament, "My son's fifteen. He's giving me all kinds of attitude when I ask for help around here. Even when I let him sleep in until six in the morning, he still fights me over getting up. Most folks I know are running into the same trouble. It must be that teenager thing."

Right. Like almost all parents everywhere for millennia, that father saw the teen years as a positive, not a disaster waiting to happen. His kids were bigger, stronger, more competent. Adolescence wasn't a rocky parenting stage to be weathered. It was welcomed. The idea that "older is harder" didn't cross Dad's mind—or, if it did, it was more than balanced by "older is more helpful."

The Anti-Parents

Our culture has birthed a cruel relative to rebellion: rejection. While rebellion is typically linked to adolescence, rejection can continue through the teens into adulthood. It is a much longer departure from a parent's guidance, an embracing of alternative, often antagonistic, ways of thinking and living. Fortunately, not all rejection is lifelong, but while it persists, it creates distress and feelings of failure for parents, who wonder, "Who is this person I raised?"

Movers and Shapers

Who or what is fomenting this rebellion turned rejection? Those who speak through the cyber sphere, media, entertainment, and education. They are the movers and shapers of our cultural mores. They extol with vigor the "progressive" ways to view values, religion, and life. They pronounce Mom, Dad, or both to be moral throwbacks, out of touch, living in last week.

Two professors, Robert Lichter and Stanley Rothman, in the 1980s conducted a bombshell survey. They asked 240 members of prestigious media—journalism, television, movies—about their political and social views.[1] Some highlights (though a better word might be "lowlights"): 45 percent of media elite considered themselves atheist or agnostic, compared with 9 percent of Americans; 6 percent of the media establishment attended church weekly, and 89 percent seldom or never, while weekly church attendance among the general population was 42 percent (it's roughly similar today), with only 25 percent seldom or never attending.

When asked if abortion at any time of pregnancy should be legal, 94 percent of those surveyed said yes. Is adultery acceptable? Media—55 percent: yes.

---

[1] S. Robert Lichter, Stanley Rothman, and Linda S. Lichter, *The Media Elite* (Bethesda, MD: Adler and Alder, 1986).

Is television critical of traditional and religious values? 80 percent: no. Too much sex on television? 70 percent: no. Too much violence? 40 percent: no.

Regarding television's elite, Lichter and Rothman state, "They are not in it just for the money. They seek to move their audience toward their own version of the good society." They emphasized that the political, social, and moral outlook of those who dwell in the upper echelons of the media does not remotely align with those of the typical American. They wholeheartedly disputed the media's claim that it merely reflects society's values and does not reshape them.

Lichter and Rothman looked at media attitudes of two generations ago. Their downward moral slide, it would be hard to dispute, has only gained momentum.

In 2006, the Media Research Center surveyed two thousand Americans, ages eighteen and older, representing a wide range of views on religion, politics, and media.[2] Among their many findings: "Adults who perceive moral decline in America consider the media the second greatest influence on moral values in our culture, exceeded only by the family." Sixty-four percent believed that the media dramatically shapes cultural morals. Only 7 percent said they do not.

"People who adhere to traditional moral values are more likely to believe the media are a major influence ... at seventy-three percent." Hollywood specifically as a major influence: 82 percent.

"The consensus is overwhelming: Any way you measure it, Americans from virtually every demographic category agree that the media, both entertainment and news, are undermining moral values." Badly.

---

[2] *The Media Assault on American Values*, Culture and Media Institute Special Report, Media Research Center, https://www.mrc.org/special-reports/media-assault-american-values.

The Anti-Parents

You don't need to read all the surveys to be convinced that the media and entertainment are radically at odds with parents trying to raise moral, responsible persons. It pervades our experience. It's coming at us and our families from every broadcasted direction.

My college-age son, Peter, said to me, "Dad, you're one voice telling me how to live. There are thousands out there criticizing you and telling me their way is better." So far, my one voice has been louder. Either that, or Peter doesn't want to cough up his own tuition.

Seeping Vapor

Some years ago, a movie called *The Fog* wafted into theaters. Its plot depicted malevolent forces inhabiting a virulently threatening ocean fog. Overcoming all attempts to seal it out, it diffused through the tiniest of cracks in any building.

The culture's voices are like this fog. They seep in, probing for the tiniest gap, breaching the protective surroundings of the home. Sophisticated and seductive, their stamina is limitless.

Is the only surefire defense to flee them? To head for the Arctic, the Sahara, the Himalayas? Suppose one did: How long before cell towers and the Internet would follow, if they aren't there already? The acceleration of technology is inescapable. And while it can move much of life upward, it can move much of family life downward, or at the least toward new terrain that is trickier to navigate. Technology itself is not the primary villain: It's the ugly stuff it invites and carries.

When Peter was in his mid-teens, he and a buddy were walking down our driveway. Looking out a window, I teasingly yelled, "Hey, you kids, get off my driveway!" At which Peter turned to his friend and cried, "Run! It's old man Ray."

This book will not be in the caricatured voice of the reclusive neighborhood curmudgeon, bemoaning the now and living in the then. Rather, this book will respect the culture when it respects you, the loving and conscientious parent, but will oppose it when it opposes you. My intent is to raise your awareness of the forces undercutting you and to build your confidence to resist them and, whenever possible, to render them allies rather than adversaries.

In the end, if you're not standing stronger, then you can walk all over my lawn. Just stay out of the flower beds.

Re-Solve

The culture has a message for parents: We don't like the way you are raising your kids. We don't think like you, believe like you, or act like you. You are so yesterday. We have all the means to mold your child in our image—a much more attractive image. And we're experts at wielding those means.

Don't underestimate the pervasiveness and persuasiveness of popular culture. From outside and inside your home, it can laud its ways and scorn yours.

You have the power to diminish its power. You have vigilance, supervision, resolve. Most of all, you have love. You love your child; the culture doesn't.

The culture thinks its way is the better way for your child to live. You know better.

2

Confront or Conform

"Do the culture's prevailing values help or hinder your parenting?" Parents answer "hinder" over "help" by about ten to one. Most see the culture's reigning morality—if that is the right word—as either unfriendly or downright hostile to their own.

"Hostile" is the chosen word among those of religious faith. They are watching the chasm between their beliefs and the culture's widen. As society pushes God further to its fringes, it is the youth who feel the distance most.

More millennials (ages eighteen to thirty-four) now live together than marry. The majority of their children are born out of wedlock. Well over half of college students stop practicing the religion of their childhood. While 26 percent of millennials claim no religion, among those youngest—ages eighteen to twenty-four—the figure rises to over one-third.

The new no-religion religion preaches that God—should He be allowed to exist—is at best stifling, at worst cruel. Either way, He's obsolete. Meanwhile, the culture everywhere advertises its up-to-the-minute program for good—I mean "acceptable"—living. And it has no shortage of venues to push its product.

Raising Upright Kids in an Upside-Down World

One in a Hundred

What would you most want to say about your child when he's twenty-two? Would it be, "Compared with a lot of others his age, I think he's doing okay. No drugs, no legal trouble, no emotional struggles." In short, a young adult with no major problems.

Or would it be, "He's a great kid—caring, mature, responsible. I think he's one in a hundred." My experience is that ninety-nine of a hundred parents hope to say the latter. How, then, does one move from hope to reality?

It starts by being willing to be a one-in-a-hundred parent. It means reaching higher than most—in love, in time, in standards, in supervision. It means protecting your child longer from soul-assaulting external influences. It means granting liberties based upon your child's moral maturity and not his age or the freedoms of his peer group. Overall, it means being resolved, whenever and however, to be countercultural.

It means also knowing you will be misunderstood, not only by your children—you can expect that—but by other parents, perhaps even your own. You are confronting, not conforming to, the fashionable trends. And for that, you'll endure ongoing questions and critiques. To stand strong, which may mean sometimes standing alone, you'll need a thicker, stiffer spine.

Will you be reassured with comments like "I wish I had your confidence. You don't seem shaken by everybody else's opinion. How do you do it?"

Not likely. As your children move through childhood, however, the picture will become clearer, especially to those who at one time couldn't grasp why you were the parent you were. Your children's character will reveal the wisdom of your ways.

Two realities are colliding. One: Many, if not most, parents know that the culture is not on their side. Two: Many parents are nonetheless allowing the culture to have major influence over their family. Why the inconsistency?

Culture Smog

I attended college in an industrial city before the days of stricter air standards. The mammoth factories spewed nonstop pollution. Driving through it, even with all the car windows closed tight, the smog ambushed the nostrils. You would think the neighbors nearby must have needed oxygen masks. Surprisingly, they didn't. They had grown desensitized. Their noses—more precisely, their brains—had adapted and stifled the smell.

Our house is two miles from an airport. Upon our moving in, the jet noise overhead screamed at us. It was louder than my kids —well, at least the biggest jets were. Some twenty years later, the airport is busier than ever. More jets zip overhead.

What jet noise?

A sensation that continually bombards us tends to lose potency over time. Our bodies and minds filter it. Sometimes that's to our benefit. Sometimes it's not. This protection can numb us to things we'd be better off to perceive. So it is with cultural messages: They are the noise surrounding us, infusing our everyday.

Advertising is one example. It saturates our eyes and ears, hawking all that is necessary for a self-satisfied, pleasure-filled life. Marketers in all modes—television, social media, print, clothes, shoes, bags, mugs, pens—pitch their products to every person more than five thousand times per day—and that was in 2007.[3] Much, if not most, of this noise does not register. It zips through our day. Still, some of it does. Marketing 101: Repetition for result.

---

[3] Louise Story, "Anywhere the Eye Can See, It's Likely to See an Ad," *New York Times,* January 15, 2007, https://www.nytimes.com/2007/01/15/business/media/15everywhere.html.

Raising Upright Kids in an Upside-Down World

A soccer referee told me of hearing music loaded with vulgar, sexually graphic lyrics pouring from the field booth onto the stands during halftime. Racing over, he expected to find teens at the helm. And there were—along with adults. The kids mouthed the words while the adults looked oblivious. When he alerted them, they looked surprised and switched the "entertainment."

A family-friendly piece of Americana—grocery-store checkout lines—once only tempted children to nag for gum and candy. Now they flaunt layers of seductive magazine covers and raunchy headlines all at a nine-year-old's eye level. Parents no longer notice. It's routine stuff. Not to kids.

Like the air that passes through our lungs, so, too, can ugly sights and sounds pass our awareness, arousing little reaction. Fortunately, our conscious mind can snap back to attention to counter what too often has become an unconscious acceptance. We can discipline ourselves to be more attuned. Vigilance is a first step in countering the culture's call.

Cultural Air Pressure

Peer pressure. It doesn't only sway teens. It sways adults as well. The parenting crowd speaks with a commanding voice, amplified by society. If culture is the air we breathe, its voice is air pressure.

Back in the old days—the late 1990s—a mother approached me after a parenting presentation. "My son is absolutely refusing to ride the school bus." Thinking perhaps the reason was anxiety, a bully, or school phobia, I asked, "How old is he?" I expected to hear a middle-school age, at the oldest. "He's seventeen." "What's his reason?" "He says, no way will he be the only senior on a bus with freshmen and sophomores." "What if you told him he has no other option? You're not giving him the car or letting someone pick him up." "His friends also refuse, and he's dug in his heels. I've never

seen him so defiant. If I push him on this, it will get really ugly."
She wanted some wise words from me to talk her son onto the bus.
I didn't have any. As long as he set the terms and she acquiesced,
the most moving logic wouldn't budge him.

Her son was traveling along with the start of a fashionable youth
movement. How it gathered so much momentum so fast prior to
social media baffles me. By some sort of shared consciousness, the
big kids diagnosed the bus juvenile.

Granted, buses may not be the sheltered sanctuaries they once
were. And a car may be more schedule flexible. Still, no-bus-for-
me-ever brings home how peer pressure can transport not only the
younger but the older.

As the mother left, I wondered how long before juniors, then
sophomores, then most any high schooler with preferred transporta-
tion would throw the bus under the bus. That's now the scene: If
your teen still rides the bus, he can pretty much sit where he wants.

Here's the point: High schoolers set the age to quit the bus.
Elementary schoolers are setting the age to get their own phones.
Patience will prod Mom or Dad, whoever's more prod-able, closer
to thinking like her peers, and thus like theirs. The kids are driving, well, the bus.

I ask parents, "If she hadn't pushed so hard and for so long,
and if more kids her age had no phone, would she have one right
now?" Standard answer: No. Persistence united with majority rule
is proving a tough duo for many parents to resist for long.

Moral Normal

+ I don't like the kind of music he listens to, but it seems
  like that's most of what's out there.
+ What she wanted to wear to homecoming made my mouth
  drop. She showed me pictures of what her classmates are

wearing. She says she'd look like a weirdo in what I think she should wear.

- He's gotten very disrespectful. My friends say it's a teen phase. They say their kids talk like that.
- His grandparents bought him a TV for his room against our wishes. They claim that most kids his age have one. (True, by the way.)

Consensus parenting. If it's common, it's normal. If it's normal, it's all right.

The new normal sets the standard. And it's being defined downward. Which movies are "must see," no matter their content. Which celebrities are to be idolized, no matter their (a)morality. Which fashions are in, no matter how lewd. Which video games are selling, no matter how vile. Which music is cutting edge, no matter how cutting or how edgy.

A parent may be alarmed by the consensus. He may want to walk or run from it yet may think himself so out of step, even with those he respects, that he is slow to move. He questions and then jettisons his judgment of what meshes with his family's standards. His vision gets clouded by second guessing.

Kids home in on a parent's self-doubt not because they're crafty creatures, though that's part of it, but because they want what they want when they want it. Don't we all? They believe, and may be so bold as to accuse outright, "How can all those parents be wrong and you be right?" A good answer: They are, and I am.

Kids think you should be guided by the numbers—if the numbers favor them, that is. Wiley would never risk naming one other kid in the Western hemisphere whose parent doesn't let him play *Raging Zombies* or who hasn't seen one minute of the wildly with-it kid cartoon show *Parents Are Major Lame*. No, that parent is as socially delayed as you are. And should you cite a few parents who *do* think like you, Wiley will just conclude that their kids are as oppressed as he is.

Suppose eighty out of one hundred parents concur that *Raging Zombies* is acceptable, rationalizing, "It's not all that bad." You're among the twenty who think it is all that bad. Were the vote to be ninety-nine "for," or at least "not strongly against," your one vote is the only vote that counts for your child. Of course, Major can't fathom why your vote should carry more weight than all those others. That is just not how an open-minded parent should operate.

However many parents call the game "not too bad" by today's slipping standards is irrelevant to you. In the words of Archbishop Fulton Sheen, "Right is right even if no one is right. Wrong is wrong even if everyone is wrong."

"Is it normal?" That question is governing more and more of our culture. It is supplanting far better questions: "Is it good? Is it right?" Mutual name calling may be "just sibling rivalry." But is name calling right? Some children can swallow a diet of rot-gut television and not get sick. Does that make the diet healthy? Most boys won't mimic the violence of vicious video games. Is watching viciousness good?

When I was fourteen, my father asked me to carry four folding chairs to the basement. What? That would take two trips. One was plenty. Tucking two chairs under each arm like crutches, I was gliding smoothly until the top step. As I stepped down, the chairs levered me off the floor, catapulting me Superman-like above ten steps. I touched nothing but air until I met the concrete floor. Except for a bruised ego—I did get all four down in one trip, so to speak—I was unhurt. Was that fast descent good for me? How many more such dives could I take before sustaining real damage?

"There's a lot worse out there." Is that the supreme measuring stick? "She's a good kid; she can deal with it." Perhaps, but at what cost? "In the end, he should be okay." Even if so, what about the meantime?

"It won't hurt them" is a feeble rationale for permitting something that, even if it does no serious harm, does little, if any, good. It can be another way of saying, "Supervising this takes too much effort." If I can reassure myself that kids are naturally resilient to cultural toxins, I won't have to be quite so vigilant.

Children stand ready to assure you that they can handle what their peers can't. "You should see what most of the kids at school get away with. And they're allowed to do way more than I am." Translation: I deserve the same amount of rope, or more, than other kids my age because I act as good as or better than they do.

Your rope's length is not measured against others'. It is *yours*. You are the judge of what to allow when, and how much rope is released or withdrawn.

Generation Transformation

"Every generation thinks things are worse now than when they were kids." That is, the idea that society is in decline is nothing new. Older folks have always thought the younger to be morally sloppier.

This notion is flawed on several levels. First, "every generation" is hyperbole. "Every" really means "the last several." Hundreds of prior generations saw few, if any, cultural changes from one generation to the next. Whatever beliefs and practices evolved did so slowly. The pace of transformation was glacial compared with the present. High-speed cultural evolution (revolution?) is a very recent phenomenon.

Second, the cultural novelties of a few generations ago now look pretty benign. In many minds, Elvis and the Beatles personified pop-culture decline. Yet, for all his on-stage kinetics, Elvis did nothing remotely resembling the lewd, semipornographic displays of current performing idols. And along with rock and roll, he also sang gospel songs.

Despite their mop-haired, anti-crew-cut style, the Beatles initially performed in suits, and not one of their top songs contained vulgar lyrics. They were the undisputed music kings of their day. The undisputed music kings of our day spout lyrics that curse, revile, and sexually demean.

Third, today's technology can rocket any nutty notion to anyone, anywhere, at the speed of light. The journalist Edgar R. Murrow observed, "Just because your voice reaches halfway around the world doesn't mean you are any smarter than when it reached only to the end of the bar." Anybody's voice—wise or foolish, good or bad—can now travel the globe.

A colleague once asserted that every generation has its techno bogeyman. Three generations ago, television was forecast to be the ruin of the young. Then came the computer to reshape their brain. The most recent menace is social media. Each advance, he said, is born, has its day, and then yields to the new kid.

True, new technologies enter the scene, but they don't always exit. They unite, partnering with pop culture to guide the attitudes of those most attracted to them—the youth. In short, the bogeyman becomes bogeymen.

It's comforting to think, "This too shall pass." After all, what our parents and grandparents thought was so bad now seems a bit overblown. We were yesterday's kids, and we steered our way into responsible adulthood. Our kids can do likewise.

The parallel isn't exact, unfortunately. Technology can now move minds by the millions. It is altering the social landscape faster than both young and old can adapt.

Thinking that it's no different now than it has always been can foster complacency. A sense of well-placed urgency will go far to help our children navigate what we never had to.

Re-Focus

You don't need to be a one-in-a-hundred parent to raise a one-in-a-hundred child. And being a one-in-a-hundred parent doesn't guarantee you'll raise a one-in-a-hundred child. But it definitely puts you and your child on course toward that outcome.

Consensus parenting can misguide you badly. Being a great parent means routinely ignoring the consensus that says what to allow your child when. It means a willingness to be misunderstood. It means walking confidently in your family's beliefs and morals.

What the majority says is the new normal may not be good, right, or moral. It may not even be normal. "Is it good?" and "Is it right?" are the far better questions to ask. They are invaluable guides to raising a child who is exceptional at age twenty-two.

3

Culture Phobia

I once listened to a counselor in a meeting authoritatively intone, "Of course, we all know that teens will rebel if a parent's standards are too high." Had I been feeling more rebellious, I would have countered, "We all don't know that. All teens don't rebel against high standards. Some rise to meet them." I was tempted to add, "That's a cultural cliché." Instead, my adult stifled my inner adolescent.

Of all the confidence-corroding, authority-assaulting, morally misguided notions flung dogmatically toward parents, "high standards risk rebellion" gets my vote for being among the worst. How's that for sensitive shrinkspeak?

When experts talk like this, what kind of standards do they mean? Academic, sports, music, chess, ancient Semitic translation? Yes, a parent can push too hard, living through his child and building up his own ego with his child's performance.

Unfortunately, this warning isn't always limited to competence or skills. It can even refer to a child's character—that is, to moral standards. Leave room for values negotiation, it says, or else Angela will despair under the pressure to reach too far upward.

In a broader sense, this cliché also refers to cultural character, basically counseling parents to give in to it. Parent too hard against it, and you are courting not only rebellion but full rejection when Angela is finally free from your narrow ideals and can follow a looser moral code.

This caution finds a face in the stereotype of the preacher's kid, whom everyone—except his parents—knows is the sneakiest, most weaselly in the congregation. If you recall the TV series *Leave It to Beaver*, think of Eddie Haskell. Nodding "yes" to his parents' direction, he acts "no," all the while gliding under their radar.

Truth is, most preachers' kids model their parents' standards. Only a minority don't. Stereotypes survive by the exceptions that fit them.

Standing Strong

High standards are not absolute. They are relative to surrounding norms. That is: High standards compared with what? Any standard can look lofty when compared with a slipping one. If the norm is unhealthy, then what departs from the norm may be quite healthy.

It was once unquestioned: Living and giving strong morals is a parental prerogative and priority. It is fuzzy morals, not definite ones, that lead to poor living. Only of late has that thinking been challenged. The counselor in that meeting was echoing contemporary education. And no one there disagreed with her—out loud anyway.

Such counsel can dissolve your resolve. After all, Dorothy already thinks she has the Wicked Witch of the West for a mother or Attila the Hun for a father. So, it feels as if you'll only bolster that image by seeming "too rigid" or "too unreasonable" or "too controlling"—standard allegations leveled at strong parents. You may be none of these, yet still be so called, not only by Dorothy but by other parents or professionals.

A mother told me of attending a teen pool party. Nearing dark, the hostess asked parents to call their kids from the pool. Several walked to the pool's edge and commenced to negotiate. Mom recalled, "I motioned with my hand for my two girls to climb out, and they immediately did. Later I found out we were the talk of the party." "Because they thought you were a parenting goddess?" I asked. "I wish. They wondered what I must do at home to make my daughters so afraid of me." Her girls were not viewed as willingly cooperative, but as automatons complying solely from intimidation. Good discipline looks "too strict" when contrasted with wobbly discipline.

Sting, your thirteen-year-old son, wants to attend a concert with five classmates. By today's criteria, the concert is benign. The band, Probation Violation, faces only two felony charges and a pending drug probe. All the other parents have said, "Okay." You've said, "Not okay." Sting is years too young; no parents are within earshot (i.e., two miles); the scene is just too crazy. You are singing solo.

Some experts—probably those without thirteen-year-olds—would instruct: Set up a win-win. Let Sting take a cell phone. If he doesn't yet have one—another sign of your intransigence—let him borrow his buddy's. He can text you on Snake's phone between songs. (Uh-huh.) Maybe Snake's dad could tag along, watching from out of sight with binoculars. Should the concert still be a no-go, how about a compromise? Sting can attend two movies of his choice with Snake and Conan. Or maybe, since you're the only parent limiting his child's socializing, talk to the other parents. Seek their reasons. Get a consensus.

My advice? Be wary of consensus parenting. All too often, it is synonymous with weak parenting.

Granted, if a parent is *autocratic*, with a "my way or the highway" style, he does invite Sly to slide around his expectations. The saying has some merit: "Rules without relationship risk rebellion."

There is a radical difference, however, between warm, strong parenting and cold, strong parenting. Where love inspires the rules, more often than not Sly will come to see with 20/20 hindsight what he didn't see with 20/200 foresight a few years prior. Who knows? He may even raise his kids by what is moral and not just normal.

Rebellious Resentment

A mother lamented that as her daughters were becoming teens, she was becoming more anxious. Their dress, social media preoccupation, opposite-sex attractions—all were moving too fast for her liking. "Who or what is keeping you from slowing things down?" I asked. "My husband." While she was willing to endure her daughters' wrath over decelerating their social speedometer, he wasn't. He feared that if he didn't match the pace of peer liberty, the girls would become resentful. He didn't want to lose their approval, even for a short while.

Anxiety is among the most common reasons parents move with the crowd, even when they'd really rather not. In our over-analyzing child-rearing climate, they get nervous about provoking potential distress. "What if" questions gnaw at them. What if he gets resentful? What if he distrusts me? What if he becomes a social outcast? What if she lies and sneaks? What if she rejects everything we believe?

In the most loving home, a "What if" can certainly happen—*temporarily*. As long as children think they know better than parents, disagreements over what is allowed when and how often will arise. But disagreement does not equal discontent. In fact, disagreement can be a sign of good parenting. If your kids always like you, that means you're raising them the way they like. And that's not smart.

Whenever you change your mind, let it be because you reassessed, and not because somebody or somebodies reassessed for you. Standing firm in what you hold to be true is the best path to one day behold a young adult who is firm in those truths.

Culture Phobia

Overprotective?

A cultural concoction that is swirling around parents these days has attained mantra status: "You can't protect them forever. It's a real world out there. They need to learn how to deal with it."

Of course you can't protect them forever. Who said anything about infinity? Yes, the world is real. As opposed to what other kind? And yes, they do need to learn how to deal with it. But when?

Few parents called "overprotective" by the culture are actually cocooning their children from life. Neither are they child-rearing bulldozers, plowing aside every emotional bump or rock. Rather, they are adding a few more years of childhood, while subtracting a few years of early adulthood. And for that, they are looked upon at the least as misguided, and at the worst as psychologically crippling. They are challenging "conventional wisdom"—now there's an oxymoron.

Who is better able to deal with the real world: a well-raised ten-year-old or a well-raised fourteen-year-old? Postponing the day of moral testing does not postpone a child's maturing; it affords him more time to study for the test.

As a college freshman, my son Andrew was assigned a controversial moral topic in a composition class. Knowing his professor's bias, he nevertheless challenged it. Had he been given a similar assignment as a high school freshman, neither his thoughts nor his confidence would have been as ready. I assured Andrew that if his grade suffered for not parroting the expected ideological line, our financial support wouldn't drop one dollar. In fact, it could go up.

My grandfather wouldn't have known exactly what "overprotective" meant. Or, if he did and had the term lobbed his way, he would have said "Thank you." Overprotecting ranked high on his daddy-do list. He knew the day would come soon enough when he couldn't protect his children anymore.

"Protective" is, like "standards," a culturally dependent term. A "sheltered" ten-year-old of today has smelled more social pollution than a typical fourteen-year-old of my grandfather's day. A parent now has to work sooner and harder to minimize the infiltration. You may be not at all overprotective: You just look so compared with those who are underprotective.

Worldliness is not maturity. In fact, they are opposed: Premature worldliness delays maturity. It can make a youngster less equipped to deal with the *real* real world. Indeed, innocence is one mature quality necessary for living in that real world.

The "S" Word

No parents hear "overprotective" more often than those who home-school. And they generally don't dispute the label! They readily accept it, asserting that their goal is not only to educate but also to guard against unwanted and untimely influences.

"What about their socialization?"—more often an objection than a question. It prompts me to ask, "What exactly does that mean?" (Just like a shrink.) Does it mean being taught how to live well with others? That is, and always will be, a parent's role. Or, does it mean absorbing the social ground rules of a group of classmates? The latter, it could be argued, is *one part* of a child's socialization, but a very small part. The "S" question—as homeschoolers call it—was never asked of parents prior to universal schooling. How were all those generations socialized?

Homeschooled kids don't live on Saturn. Most live in places surrounded by people, with whom they talk and mingle and inter-act. Their world is not a social vacuum.

Bill Bennet, a former secretary of education, was asked for an answer to the "S" question. He succinctly replied, "Socialization to what?" In other words, socialization has to be defined—when, where, and by whom. One mother, when confronted with, "Aren't you concerned for their socialization?" simply replied, "That's why I homeschool."

"Part of growing up is learning the skills for getting along with all kinds of people. Children need to experience the push and pull of human contact." True, but how are those skills learned? Through peers, whose push and pull may be forward or backward? Or through adults, who may be a little bit better at instilling qualities such as kindness, tolerance, and responsibility—the core of socialization?

Can a youngster be so sequestered that he becomes a square peg in a social round hole? Could too much sheltering backfire so that one day, freshly liberated, he'll rush headlong into all sorts of wrongdoing? (Note: This is a variant of "High standards risk rebellion.")

Certainly one can take the protective impulse to the point of self-sabotage. A vice is often a virtue taken to extreme. Research, however, finds that homeschooled children are anything but socially short-changed. Their self-image is as solid, or more so, than their nonhomeschooled counterparts. They are at ease around both children and adults. They are more civically minded, likelier to volunteer, join organizations, and vote. Overall, they report high levels of contentment.

One needn't homeschool to raise a great kid. That is not the message here. Rather, it is to debunk the main myth leveled at those thought to be the epitome of protective parents.

If you refuse to accept the culture's ever-more-lax rules about what to let your children see, hear, and do, it's a given: You will be called protective. And it won't be meant as a compliment. One mother, when so challenged, answered with, "I hope I am. I want to give my children a childhood while they're still children."

Re-Turning

As the culture ever more stubbornly refuses to protect children, your protection will be countercultural. You are not agreeing with the norm. You look misguided. But if those around you are traveling in a bad direction, you're wise to travel a different way.

You're controlling. Yes, you strive to control the pace and spread of influences that can hurt your child.

You're overprotective. Compared with those who are underprotective, the label fits you. What's more, it's welcomed. Your child needs more protection than you did when you were his age.

If someday your child is pulled toward the culture's ways more than yours, let it be because he climbed over your gate, not because you opened it.

4

Locked in Your Cell

A recent documentary highlighted modern inventions that have most transformed our lives. Ranking number one was the smartphone. Slightly larger than a deck of cards, it fuses phone, radio, television, and computer. Among its mind-numbing capabilities are split-second contact with nearly anyone anywhere, access to the world's knowledge, unlimited social connections, instant media, and endless entertainment.

The smartphone would also be at the top of my list of innovations that have transformed family life. It has reshaped childhood and parenthood in ways unseen a mere twenty years ago. Introduced as a phone, albeit with a global cord, it swiftly evolved into an all-purpose, well, *everything*. The transformation has been nothing short of disorienting.

Even so, my call is not to pitch all phones into the lake or the toilet—though I do see circumstances where that is the wisest option. The smartphone isn't about to say goodbye, at least not until the next unpredictable techno leap makes it go the way of the rotary phone. It is so fully woven into the fabric of our everyday that we not only want it there: We are convinced we *need* it there.

Like any potent piece of progress, the smartphone requires handling with great care. A chain saw is really good at cutting the time

27

and energy needed to remove a tree. It is really bad in the hands of a ten-year-old. Nothing has ever been more effective than the Internet at bringing the best minds of humanity into one's own mind. Nothing has also been more effective at bringing the worst of humanity into one's soul. What good or ill the phone brings depends on the maturity, psychological stability, and self-control of its handler. In short, *who* uses it *for what, when,* and *how often.*

Turning Point

Jean Twenge has been studying differences across generations for some twenty-five years. Writing in the *Atlantic,* she stated that generational characteristics, for the most part, shift gradually. Around 2012, though, she saw abrupt changes in teens' emotions and behavior. "In all my analyses—some dating back to the 1930s—I had never seen anything like it."

What happened in 2012? The percentage of teens with smartphones exploded past 50 percent. "The arrival of the smartphone has radically changed every aspect of teenagers' lives, from the nature of their social interactions to their mental health.... These trends appear among teens poor and rich; of every ethnic background; in cities, suburbs, and small towns. Where there are cell towers, there are teens living their lives on their smartphone."[4]

Among other findings: Twelfth graders in 2015 socialized personally with friends less often than eighth graders in 2009. From 2000 to 2015, the percentage of teens who got together with friends every day dropped some 40 percent. Without exception, more

---

[4] Jean M. Twenge, "Have Smartphones Destroyed a Generation?" Atlantic (September 2017), https://www.theatlantic.com/magazine/archive/2017/09/has-the-smartphone-destroyed-a-generation/534198/.

screen-time is linked to less happiness, more feelings of being "left out," and increased likelihood of depression.

Time Warp

For nearly all of history, science and technology crept along, inching forward over centuries. And progress wasn't always predictable: It moved forward and backward from place to place and culture to culture. The sluggish pace gave successive generations time to adapt. Techno progress didn't overwhelm the family order.

In college, I came across a statistic predicting that the sum of human knowledge would double every eleven years. How snail-like. Recent estimates are that it doubles in less than a year.

Technology fuels itself. Its growth is not linear but exponential. Shedding the math lingo, this means it doesn't advance at a steady rate. Instead, it gallops ahead ever faster. To borrow a phrase from *Star Trek*, "Take us ahead Warp Factor Four, Mr. Sulu." Or, "Go really fast."

Early cell phones were still just phones, though a great leap forward in communication. To my grandfather, they would have been the stuff of science fiction. Dick Tracey, the comic-strip detective of his day, talked face-to-face with others via a wristwatch-style device. Most everybody then knew such a thing was somewhere in the far-off future.

The "simple" cell phone had its day, almost literally a day, before it was ousted by the smartphone. The unchecked enthusiasm for all its predicted benefits muffled any voices calling for caution. Such voices risked sounding a bit like nervous reactionaries wanting to cling to simpler times. Only of late has a gathering group—researchers, professionals, parents—talked more boldly of the negatives of overuse: social isolation, turning inward, emotional distress, not to mention moral dangers.

Raising Upright Kids in an Upside-Down World

Parents have been caught in a techno time warp. The smartphone infused itself into the cultural psyche before its potential downsides were foreseen. Many accepted the notion: "It's progress, and progress is good. What could go wrong?" Only gradually are parents coming to recognize that all is not okay with smartphones.

Age Slide

Pew Research reported that in 2009, by age thirteen 73 percent of children had a personal phone. Five years earlier, the percentage was 34.[5] Another early 2010s survey found that 56 percent of kids between eight and twelve had a phone, with another 21 percent under age eight.[6] Surveys overall agree that the average age of first phone possession falls between ten and twelve.

Coupled with age regression is phone progression. No longer are most phones "dumb phones." (Amazing how quickly such a communication breakthrough gets called dumb.) Kids don't want dumb; they want smart, with all the up-to-the-second, must-have innovations. One study noted that over 90 percent of teens spend time on the Internet through their phones.[7]

---

[5] David Bredehoft, "Who Says Kids More Overindulged and Spoiled Today?" Raising Likable, Responsible, Respectful Children in an Age of Overindulgence, November 15, 2017, http://www.overindulgence.org/blog/are-kids-more-overindulged.html. From data compiled by CTIA, a wireless industry trade group.

[6] Amanda Lenhart, Rich Ling, Scott Campbell, and Kristen Purcell, "Teens and Mobile Phones," Pew Research Center, January 3, 2014, https://www.pewinternet.org/2010/04/20/chapter-one-the-basics-of-how-teens-acquire-and-use-mobile-phones/.

[7] Amanda Lenhart, "Teens, Social Media, and Technology Overview 2015," Pew Research Center, February 1, 2016, https://www.pewinternet.org/2015/04/09/teens-social-media-technology-2015/.

What do these statistics mean for parents?

- During early adolescence, the brain is neurologically juvenile in judgment, impulse control, and ability to foresee consequences. Cell phones and immaturity can make for all manner of unanticipated bad outcomes.
- Delay granting Alexander a phone until he reaches the ripe old age of fourteen, and you are in a fast-dwindling minority. Delay until sixteen, and you are a pre-Bell relic. "Relic," though, doesn't mean wrong.
- With the masses on her side, Harmony can't fathom why you still won't get with them. The only explanation, as she sees it, is that you're closed-minded. It's her duty to open your mind, no matter how long that takes.
- Once upon a time, a parent could confidently dismiss the line that "All my friends are allowed" or "Other parents think it's okay." He knew Addy was spinning the reality. He knew other parents who thought as he did. But Addy isn't spinning much anymore. She is citing facts. Every kid she knows *does* have a state-of-the-art phone.

Of course, whatever the reality, the only reality that matters is "our family, not theirs."

Age Entitlement

Kids believe that with age come rights. "I'm sixteen; I'm old enough to drive." Translation: "I am entitled to drive." In most states, sixteen is the minimum age to independently operate a vehicle. It's not the age it *must* happen. A parent has the license to decide that.

"I'm eighteen; I can make my own decisions." Not all of them. It depends on where you live. The day after my oldest son, Andrew, turned eighteen, I spoke with him. "Andrew, you are now legally an adult. That means you don't have to follow our rules anymore. You can set your own. You can stay out as late as you wish, spend your money however, go to church if you feel like it ..." As I rambled on, Andrew started to smile. Not because he was thinking, "All right, Pop is getting it. He's moving into the twenty-first century." No, because he knew where I was heading: "Of course, if you do want to make all your own rules, you will also have to find your own place to live." Adult freedom must not have been so appealing to Andrew. He stayed home until he got married, when he still couldn't do as he pleased all the time.

Driving age and legal age are fixed numbers. The phone custody age isn't. It's fluid and moving younger. It has to bottom out somewhere eventually, but there's no sign of that yet. The *Journal of Pediatrics* reported that up to 97 percent of children age four and under interact with some kind of handheld device, and 20 percent of one-year-olds are able to navigate a tablet. Now I know where to turn for help with mine.

Kids don't consider the phone a privilege to earn; they consider it an entitlement of age, an age that is arriving ever earlier.

It's basic statistics: The further you are from the average, the less company you have. It's basic psychology: The further you are from the average, the less others think like you. As the average phone age now hovers between ten and eleven, with each year your child remains phoneless, you'll confuse more people. "Why don't you give him a phone? He's a good kid." "Everyone her age has one; it's how they communicate." "How long are you going to wait? Isn't he getting pretty pushy by now?"

The mean has social clout. It gathers followers. But you are wise to ignore it. If Marlin's parents jump in the lake ...

Sometimes a grandparent will force a parent's hand. She will buy her grandchild a phone, thinking that without one, he will be an oddball among her peers. The parent afterward will confide to me, "If it were up to me, he wouldn't have one." I ask, "Who's it up to?"

Age is not the major consideration in granting a phone. Trustworthiness is, and that may not correlate with age at all. Others know how old your child is. That's easy. Only you know his level of trustworthiness. And that's a harder judgement call.

Addiction?

Strictly defined, addiction includes three features: craving, dependence, and withdrawal. Craving is an intense desire for a substance. Dependence means needing the substance to function, and over time needing more of it to get the same effect (habituation). Withdrawal is the body's agonizing, sometimes life-threatening, reaction to stopping the substance abruptly. If "cell phone" is substituted for "substance," even the most intense cell phone habit may not reach a true addiction. Still, there are parallels.

Craving. The younger the child when he starts wrangling for a phone, the more his craving builds. As a rule, kids don't push for a phone less when denied; they push more. When the craving is finally satisfied, they are anxious to recoup lost time.

Nicotine fact: The younger someone starts to smoke, the harder it is to shake the habit. Never starting is much easier than quitting. Cell phone fact: the younger someone starts on the phone, the harder to shake its hold. One's social psyche comes to crave it.

According to a *New York Times* report, teens and adults check their smartphones nearly 150 times a day. That's nine times per waking hour! One would think that the everyday calls of living would slow the rate. Pew Research, however, confirms it, finding that people eyeball their phones every 4.3 minutes. The *Times* also notes the typical number of sent and received texts per day: 150.[8]

---

[8] Jane E. Brody, "Hooked on Our Smartphones," *New York Times,* January 9, 2017.

One father told me of his daughter's text intoxication after she totaled ten thousand in one month.

A ten-country survey found that 92 percent of respondents went online daily, with 24 percent confessing "almost constantly."[9] On a recent trip to an African country, my wife saw material poverty but cell phone plenty. The siren call of the phone travels easily across cultural landscapes.

Dependence. The *Journal of Behavior Addictions* (2011) stated that 60 percent of college students called themselves "addicted," spending upward of two hours daily on Facebook. Putting similar hours into academics would go far toward a 4.0 average.

The journal also reported that 59 percent of parents use "addicted" to describe their child's phone habits.[10] Other descriptions are: attached, hooked, preoccupied, obsessed, wedded, third kidney.

To assess your child's phone dependence, ask:

- Must it always and everywhere be hooked to her? How much panic follows if it's out of reach, however briefly? (When will there be showerproof phones?)
- How much is the phone encroaching on the stuff of everyday life—schoolwork, conversations, chores, meals, driving, sleeping? Thirty-five percent of those in one survey checked their phones in the last five minutes before falling asleep.[11] Do they need to remain unconscious to let

---

[9] Lenhart, "Teens, Social Media."

[10] James Roberts, Luc Yaya, and Chris Manolis, "The Invisible Addiction: Cell-Phone Activities and Addiction among Male and Female College Students," *Journal of Behavioral Addictions* 3, no. 4 (2014): 254–265.

[11] "Global Mobile Consumer Survey: U.S. Edition," Deloitte, September 5, 2019, https://www2.deloitte.com/us/en/pages/technology-media-and-telecommunications/articles/global-mobile-consumer-survey-us-edition.html.

the phone sleep? *Back to the Family*[12] summarized the findings of a nationwide search for strong families. In essence, the survey, which took place before the widespread use of phones, asked, "How are you raising such a strong family?" Parents in these families had found, to their surprise, that their teens opened up more while riding in the car with Mom or Dad. How much conversation would happen now if Chevy started up his phone before Dad or Mom even started the car?

- How often does Celina's phone interrupt others? Is she texting while everybody else is singing "Happy Birthday" to her brother? One comedian quipped that guys with a TV remote don't want to see what's on; they want to see *what else* is on. Cell phones breed a similar mind-set: Wait, let me see who else wants my attention right now.

Phone rehab begins with the parent. Few kids will temper the habit on their own. "I'm way too into my phone. I'm going to cut back, starting tomorrow. I'll send myself a text to remind me."

A parent may observe dependency but be unsure what to do about it. She may wonder: How much is too much? Is this normal for her age? Is it a phase? What if I force a pullback? How much pushback will I get?

These questions will be answered in the next chapter. For now, begin by following your instincts. If you believe your child is too locked into his phone, reassess and reset the conditions for its use. A smart parent knows to reverse direction when her first move isn't going where she planned.

---

[12] Dr. Ray Guarendi, *Back to the Family: How to Encourage Traditional Values in Complicated Times* (New York: Villard Books, 1990).

Withdrawal. Withdrawal can be an unpleasant experience. How's that for understatement? A substance is habitually ingested. Over time, the body adjusts to its presence. Cease ingesting it abruptly, and the body will react, sometimes fiercely.

Though cell phone withdrawal may not be physical, it certainly is mental. The mind screams, "Give it back! Now!" Withholding something that is considered not a want, but a *need*, is intolerable.

Scenario: A teen misuses the phone, and the parent pulls the privilege, however temporarily. Ripley's reaction is unbelievable. It is beyond anything the parent has seen. No other discipline — grounding, loss of car, extra chores, curfew contraction — has ever evoked such fuming resistance or outright defiance. The intensity of the withdrawal reaction is directly related to the social and emotional dependence. And that is related to how long Ripley has had his phone.

While I was working in my yard, a neighbor approached and asked, "Did you see a girl walk through here?" "No," I replied, "How old is she?" "Fourteen," then, "I think my daughter just ran away," and he rushed off. Later I went to his house, asking, "Can I do anything to help?" He said, "Thanks, but we found her." I asked, "Did you take her cell phone away, and then she left?" Looking at me as if I had just performed a carnival trick, he answered, "Yes. We took it because of her grades. We took it once before, but as soon as we gave it back, they dropped. So we took it again and were shocked by how mad she got."

How did I know about the repossession? Probabilities. When a youngster regards her phone as an absolutely vital lifeline to the outside world, forced withdrawal can provoke a desperate response. Nonetheless, when a child's well-being is suffering, withdrawal may be the best medicine. But every parent knows how much a child can resist taking medicine.

Re-Evaluate

Trust your eyes. Are you watching your child's phone passion interfere with the rest of life? Is what you are seeing unsettling? Is it different from what you initially expected to see? Clearer vision leads to better parenting.

Trust your ears. Do you like your youngster's way of speaking, on and off his phone? Has his language changed for the better or for the worse? Are you hearing more or less maturity? More or less peer influence? Your ears will give you the input to take smart action.

Trust your gut. Are you sensing that, overall, the phone is not serving your child's character? Do you feel obliged to justify to young and old alike every reason why you are rethinking the phone? You have your own reasons, and they are good ones. Trust your instincts.

5

Phone Smart

My cell phone became my personal assistant some twenty-five years ago. (For the record, I was well past junior high.) It promptly proved its worth. Anywhere, anytime, I could reach out and touch home. It saved hours of returning calls parked on an answering machine. Stepping up to a smartphone added e-mail, easy texting, and Internet—all business streamliners.

My phone is a major aide. It is also a major nag. I'm not sure if it answers to me or if I answer to it.

It also has an annoying habit: It texts to me my daily phone time. My guess would've been about an hour. Turns out it's more than twice that. In my defense, I do use it for news and music. Still, I missed the mark by well over an hour. Talk about a stealth presence.

A Case for the Phone

"Her school sends out updates about everything—schedules, events, schoolwork—on the phone. They just assume all the kids have one." Everyday life pushes you toward a phone, whether you're ready or not.

Our daughter Liz was one of a handful of phone-deprived ninth graders at her school. Her track coach contacted all runners via group texts—not during a race, though I suspect some of the kids would have stopped to answer. How did Liz get her messages? They were relayed through Mom. Coach had my wife's cell number. Liz didn't like the plan. We ran well with it.

If you don't relish acting as a text clearinghouse, you could get your teen her own phone. What about one that can only call and text—not access the Internet? They still exist. Ask your third-grade niece for her old phone. Your teen would be really reluctant to pull out this relic in front of her friends. "What is that? Where did you find it? Is it illegal? Does it hurt?"

"What is your reason for giving him a phone at his age?" I ask parents. Number-one answer: "We want to always be able to contact each other." Granted, practices do run late; friends change plans; cars act up; curfews get renegotiated last minute. But if constant contact is the driving rationale, once more: Wouldn't a no-Internet phone do? Does Mercedes need to send an Instagram message: "Pick me up later"?

Safety is a parent's soft spot. Kids are acutely aware of that. It's a prized bargaining chip. While it may be your soft spot; it's not theirs. If it were, Freeman would accept any type of phone. He agrees with your motive, not your solution. A flip phone is just too juvenile.

A second option: A phone with a limited number of minutes per month. That should be plenty to handle the unexpected, though probably not enough for a prolonged plea for a curfew reprieve.

A third option: A phone limited to preferred contacts—Dad, Mom, police, pizza. Library? Right. If safety matters above all else, any phone lacking the Internet is the safest by far.

One young man accosted his father: "I'm the only one of my friends who doesn't have a phone. What if I need to call you?" Dad countered, "Since you say all your friends have phones, borrow one of theirs. You have plenty of choices."

Phone Smart

Friends by Phone

"Phones are how everybody talks with everybody now. Without a phone, how can I have any friends?" Do you realize what you're doing? According to Polly, you're socially disconnecting her. No phone equals no friends.

A mother of three girls, ages twelve, thirteen, and fifteen, chastised me for not acknowledging—so she thought—that kids phoneless at their ages would be relegated to a semicloistered existence. No question, given a phone, most kids will eagerly head down its social avenues. Does it follow that every other social avenue is then closed? School? Activities? Sports? All the connections that nurtured friendships a mere generation ago? Are they outdated? Are they no longer the most personal? (And yet, even within eye- and earshot of friends, they resort to the phone.)

After sneaking past our no-phone-after-9-p.m. rule, our seventeen-year-old daughter was grounded and had her phone repossessed. Talk about solitary confinement. Panicky, she probed for a loophole. "I was supposed to meet Sarah tomorrow. I have to let her know now I can't come." I pointed to our kitchen phone. The way she recoiled, it might as well have been a hissing king cobra. "I can't use that." "Why not?" "Because Sarah won't answer. She won't know it's me." I was just about to suggest, "Leave a voice message," when, duh, I realized her friend probably only checks texts. Voice message? How 2017.

Fast-paced lifestyles beckon, "Get on board. We'll set the speed." Barring an off-the-grid retreat to some uncharted South Pacific island, you will feel the acceleration. It is inescapable. That doesn't mean you have to move with the traffic. You still control the gas pedal and the brakes in your home.

Raising Upright Kids in an Upside-Down World

The Debate

Oral and her mother are in a van, trading words about her right to a phone. I'm in the back seat, listening and adding my own words.

ORAL: None of my friends can believe you won't let me have a phone yet. I'm the only one I know who doesn't have one. I can pay for it myself.

MOM: We've been over this a hundred times, Oral. You don't need one; you are not old enough for one; and your friends can believe anything they want.

DR. RAY: This dead-end conversation has been dialed up repeatedly in the past. Undeterred, Oral reiterates to Mom just how radically detached she is from the parenting norm—this being the cardinal sin in an adolescent's rules for life. Still, Mom keeps angling for a clear reception.

MOM: Your dad and I will decide when you are old enough. Right now you are not even close, so this isn't something you need to get worked up about.

ORAL: How old do I have to be? I am older, you know. How will you decide when I'm old enough? I get good grades; I never get in trouble; I do what you tell me. You say I have to be responsible, but it doesn't matter.

DR. RAY: With laser-like insight, Oral informs Mom that this is as old as she has ever been. The implication: I'm getting closer to the magic age, whatever that is, but you'll probably just keep moving it back anyway. Oral's prime accusation is aimed at engendering Mom's guilt and sense of fair play: "I'm a wonderful human being, and this is the thanks I get."

MOM: You are a good kid. But that doesn't mean you'll get privileges you aren't ready for yet. Being mature for your age doesn't automatically get you every freedom you want.

ORAL: So how do I get freedom? I'm doing everything I can, and it's still not good enough. You just change the rules anyway. It makes me not even want to try anymore.

DR. RAY: A veiled psychological threat: "Keep up your end of the bargain (as I've defined it), Mom, or I'll drop my end." In essence, you'll force me to reject the very maturity you say you want.

MOM: Oral, if you weren't who you are, you wouldn't have the freedoms you do have. But that doesn't mean your friends know what is good for you. As far as I'm concerned, I don't think any of them should have phones either.

ORAL: Oh, wow, Mom! I never thought of it like that. If I would just listen, I'd hear how much sense you make. That's why you're the parent, and I'm the child. It's the wisdom thing, isn't it?

DR. RAY: I confess, Oral didn't say any of that. I did. At this point in the exchange, the odds of her saying anything agreeable are slightly less than getting a cell signal on the moon. Let's return to letting Oral speak for herself.

ORAL: Oh, so now my friends are the problem? I don't see how you can think that. They all get good grades, too, and they never get in any kind of trouble. That's why their parents trust them.

DR. RAY: So there, Mom. Heard enough? Had enough? You are just not a trusting parent. So what can Mom say to make Oral understand? Not much, but she can end the debate.

MOM: Oral, we're going nowhere with all this. No matter what I say, or what reasons I give you, you won't agree. So before we both get too mad, I'm not arguing any more about a cell phone.

DR. RAY: Mom could add a post-text, employing some of Oral's reasoning. Teens hate that.

MOM: Oral, you are absolutely right. Maturity does bring privileges. And one part of maturity is accepting the rules you don't like. So if you keep nagging me about a phone, you'll be telling me you're not yet mature about all this. And the more you push, the more I will push back the cell phone age.[13]

Time Management

So Oral finally gets a phone. With fanfare, you present it during her wedding rehearsal dinner. Just joking—she gets it at her college graduation party.

Whatever her age, set your phone rules at the outset. Proactive rules make for more balanced use and less family friction than reactive ones.

Time limits. It's hard for a parent to know a youngster's time on the cell. (As I've said, it's hard for me to know my own cell time.) You can only guess by what you see and hear. Only the phone itself will provide an accurate number, and you can always check that. Of course, Alexander will counter, "I don't think that's right. It's been glitchy since I dropped it in a puddle last week."

Give an allowance. How much time is Alexander granted per day? Can he purchase additional time? By the hour? Quarter hour? Minute? How much does your day pass cost?

If Alex overspends his allowance, he loses the phone the next day. Or, set a ratio: Each half hour overrun equals one day of no phone. An hour and a half overrun would thus lead to a three-day forfeiture.

Phone-free mornings. School mornings are chaotic by nature. Phone-free mornings lessen the bedlam. They allow Newton a few more minutes to eat, talk, bicker with siblings, and find his misplaced math book. Phone or no phone, he may still run late. He's not refusing to ride the bus, is he?

---

[13] Dr. Ray Guarendi, *Winning the Discipline Debates: Dr. Ray Coaches Parents to Make Discipline Less Frequent, Less Frustrating, and More Consistent* (Cincinnati: Servant Books, 2011).

Phone-free nights. No phone after bedtime or earlier. Teachers are teaching to more and more drowsy and dozing students. One culprit is the late-night phone vigil. Phones and beds are a sleep-depriving duo. Even if Eve doesn't "send," she will "receive" from those who have no nighttime downtime. To eliminate temptation, the phone vacates the bedroom.

Grades-control phone. Not only do phones sabotage sleep; they sabotage grades. The most competent, entertaining teacher is competing with an infinity of attention-grabbing stimulation outside the classroom, and sometimes within. Grades reflect Webster's ability, or the phone is hung up. The relationship is predictable: Falling grades follow rising phone time.

Homework first. Upon walking in the door, Oxford proudly proclaims, "I got everything done at school." Five hours later, "I forgot. I've got a twenty-page paper due tomorrow morning, and I still have to call Page to find out what our topic is. She's my group partner." Trust, but verify.

Muted meals. In a nationwide survey of strong families, mealtime was jealously guarded. No extraneous background noise was allowed to intrude — no TV, no music, no headsets, no phone.[14] (Babies were permitted.) Study after study confirms the cohesive power of family meals. Phoneless tables make for more interaction as well as better etiquette.

Upon sitting down at a restaurant, diners immediately set the table with their manifold devices. Young children fixate on their games, tuning out Mom, Dad, or siblings, who don't notice, as they, too, are tuning everybody out. Wherever the table — home or away — food and conversation are the main courses, not phones.

No-phone zones. An ignored grandmother watched her grand-kids stay hooked to their phones whenever they visited. Her

[14] Guarendi, *Back to the Family.*

45

remedy: All phones are to be placed on the kitchen counter from entrance to exit. Did that shorten their visits? It actually lengthened them.

Grandma's rule suits any occasion: Grandpa's birthday, Cousin Kensey's baby shower, Christmas Eve. Tuning out one's phone when around others shows respect. It sends a compliment as well: "I like your company, and I don't need the company of my phone while I'm here."

Wherever the phone rests — counter, car, purse, pocket, tree — set it on silent. Researchers are finding that the phone's signal excites the brain. It provokes a chemical response: "I must answer. It compels me." Does the name Pavlov ring a bell?

Whatever phone rules you set, one rule is paramount: Any rule can be modified at any time. You know best how Belle's phone is affecting her time, her character, and her life. Smart parents see the unintended effects of a decision, and they adjust. The kids think you're arbitrarily changing the rules. Indeed, you are changing the rules, but not arbitrarily.

Disrespect = Disconnect

Parents regularly seek my guidance about a teen's ongoing resistance to their expectations and rules. Permeating the defiance is disrespect — arguments, surly words, sour tone, back talk, back looks.

I ask, "Does your daughter [or son] have a smartphone?" Seldom is the answer "Not yet" or "Not as long as she's acting like this." More often, it's "Yes," followed by a perplexed look that asks, "How is that related to the disrespect?"

I ask, "How long has she had a phone?" The older the child, the longer. "How long has disrespect been a problem?" The older the child, the longer. Which raises a further question: Why does a child acting this unpleasantly for this long have a phone? The explanations vary: I didn't think the two were all that related; she wasn't this uncooperative when she first got it; he's not always disrespectful; I can only imagine how disrespectful he'd get if I took his phone.

In fact, too much phone can fuel disrespect. The phone is a daily reminder of how much Gabby's friends have, do, and get. The wider the gap between their liberties and hers, the more she can feel shortchanged. So, she expresses her discontent toward the people she sees as shortchanging her.

Contrary to Gabby's belief, a phone is not a birthright. It is a privilege. And a privilege must be earned, not by being occasionally pleasant, but by being consistently so. Linking the phone to respect may result in a short-term surge of surliness. Long-term, though, Gabby should learn how to act in order to keep this precious privilege. In short, until cooperation is present, the phone isn't.

Major Misuse

A common chain of events: Parents allow a phone, albeit with mixed emotions. The culture is pushing them hard one way, parental caution the other. With surprise, they watch the phone soar to indispensable status in their child's world, causing them to wonder: Did I act too soon?

Nonetheless, they live with their doubts, as some of the phone's by-products—a twitchy attention span, social media fixation, text dramas—they consider minor; they're annoying but tolerable.

Then emerges the intolerable—major misuse. I don't mean to scare you—well, maybe a little. Nor to impugn your parenting or your child's moral makeup. I mean to alert you to unexpected possibilities.

Major misuse blindsides parents. They don't fully anticipate the phones' potential for problems. Opportunity and secrecy coupled with temptation are ready-made for trouble.

Pornography

No misuse rock parents more than a child's seeking pornography. Unfortunately, it is not rare. One survey noted that 90 percent of kids, ages eleven through nineteen, have been exposed to pornography, deliberately or accidentally. Another found that the age of first encounter roughly correlates to the age at getting one's first smartphone.

A mother stumbled upon her daughter's diary while cleaning her room. (If kids cleaned their rooms themselves ...) Maternal curiosity and instinct prompted her to begin reading. Within a few pages, emotional shockwaves hit. Her daughter was engaging in some very risky and crudely narrated behavior.

When confronted, the daughter roared into high dudgeon. "You invaded my privacy! You have no right to get into my stuff. See if I ever tell you anything again!" In less than a minute, Mom went from guardian to snoop to self-doubter: Did I pry? The diary wasn't mine. Should I be more trusting? I had no reason to be suspicious.

Now nearing extinction, diaries are slow-moving, hand-written narratives of a child's mental meanderings. In contrast, cell phones are warehouses, stored with desires, plans, activities, associates. Further, the details are far more easily hidden than a diary, even in the most land-filled bedroom.

Should you supervise only somewhat? To where a child declares—and some experts declare—are your limits? If you see or hear something unnerving, are you then permitted to act? Otherwise, are you not permitted to roam into Pandora's room, her phone, or her computer without a warrant?

The "right to privacy" makes for good laws. It makes for bad parenting. A child's right to privacy is superseded by another right: the right to safety—social and moral. Well above any right to have secrets is the right to be protected from the results of those secrets.

The Internet is a worldwide theater, filled with really good images and really bad images, really good guys and really bad guys. The really bad must be rendered fully, not partially, off-limits. Fortunately, the Internet can police itself. All kinds of technological high walls are available to safeguard your kids. Build them. Otherwise, a phone or a computer may not be a chain saw in the hands of a four-year-old. It may be more like a machine gun.

Picture This

The pictures are not of sunsets or puppies, but of states of undress. This is "sexting." The images may be solicited or unsolicited, of oneself or others, with or without permission.

More young people see sexting as "no big deal," just a harmless way to titillate or to enhance a liaison. Not only is it morally suspect and personally risky: Depending on the content, it can be illegal. What may have started as "for your eyes only" can ultimately be used to embarrass, bully, or blackmail. Once that picture zooms into cyberspace, who knows where it could head? It's no longer "for your eyes only."

If your youngster tells you about an unsolicited sext, the sender's parent or parents need to be told immediately—no matter how much your child objects. It's surprising how often parents hesitate to do so, for fear of their own child's reaction or the reaction of her peers. You're "snitching," a cardinal sin for many youth. One thing is near certain: The receiver is not the first person to get a sext from this sender.

Raising Upright Kids in an Upside-Down World

Should you somehow discover you weren't told about a sext, for any reason—not to "betray," or to store the image, or to quietly delete it—the matter is serious. Innocently receiving a sext is not a phone felony; deception about it is.

A sent sext results in the phone being sent into exile. For how long? Until you can be reasonably assured it won't happen again. That could be quite a while.

Young Love

When speaking to a group of parents, I regularly cite a study from the 1980s: If a child has a first date between the ages of eleven and thirteen, they have a 90 percent chance of being sexually active as a senior in high school. First date at age fourteen leads to a 50 percent chance. First date at age sixteen: 20 percent.

Some in the audience gasp, silently asking, "Who would allow a child to date at age eleven?" As "date" was used thirty years ago—to "go out" with someone—few parents. As the word is currently used, by the young anyway, many parents.

The phone is the new, fashionable courtship venue. Through texts and social media, a "love" link is forged. By the time a parent detects it, if she does, Juliet is convinced hers is real romance, central to her happiness.

Most parents talk first with Juliet, hoping to get her to rethink the liaison. Should she not be agreeable (surprise!), a parent has to ponder a default option: Curtail the contact by curtailing the phone.

Will this foster a "forbidden fruit" attraction? Couldn't it nudge Juliet toward more stealthy contacts?

Fruit hanging just out of reach can look the sweetest to young eyes. Someone with older eyes (read: parent) may have to hang it farther up the tree. Much that looks delicious to the young can make them sick.

Sometimes a cell romance cools on its own, more quickly if there are few other points of contact. It comes and goes without a parent sensing that it was ever there. Such is the complexion of many phone-fed flings.

Limiting Juliet's online presence to daylight hours can also cool a phone romance, as it routinely gains heat in the dark seclusion of one's room. Then, too, if Romeo has unlimited phone time, he may weary of Juliet's restricted hours and move on to freer pastures.

Faking the Grade

Schools have diverse policies on phones. Some sequester them in lockers from the beginning to the end of the school day. Some permit them in backpacks only. Some grant them seats at students' desks, under the theory that phones boost learning.

Teachers are learning, however, that any potential in-class gain is more than offset by complications. The phones are sabotaging instruction and grades. In addition to the tempting distractions of texting and social media, they promote cheating.

Monitoring a class of test-taking kids has become a test for the teachers. Phones are concealed ingeniously, with surreptitious searching for answers. Kids take pictures of the test for later sharing or selling. Teachers are forced to compose two or more exams over the same material, working to level the grading field. A teacher friend, when he sees students staring downward at a hidden phone, asks, "What is so interesting about your lap?"

Those who won't cheat feel cheated by those who will. They know that phone sleights of hand result in unfairly inflated grade points, which in turn lowers their own standing.

What if your school permits classroom phones and you think that's not at all smart? You could threaten Belle with sitting behind her in class. Do that, and she might just shatter her phone to keep you miles from school. That would solve the problem. More feasible, ask the teacher(s) to collect Belle's phone, to be returned at class's end, or better yet, at day's end.

Not all teachers will confiscate a phone, and not all administrations will support that. Backup option: Request an e-mail or a text from the teacher, should Oxford's phone surface during class. If it does, no phone to school for one week. Second offense: No phone to school for one month.

The good news: More teachers are more grateful to have an ally helping them resist the invasion of the phone people.

Major Forfeiture

"How long should he lose the phone for doing something this bad?" ask parents. My reply: "Your call." And to think, I get paid for such expertise. To give parents a little more for their money, I add, "My experience is that parents are generally too quick to return a phone, hoping that its loss, however temporary, will teach the lesson and ensure that nothing similar happens again."

Rather than, "How long with no phone?", the better question may be, "Was the phone returned too soon?" Has Faith shown herself able or willing to be trusted with this far-reaching privilege? Her misconduct may dictate the answer.

The first time major misuse comes to light is typically not the first time it has happened. The privacy of phones allows duplicity to go unnoticed for some time.

Good News

My calls for tight vigilance could make it sound as if every youngster is only one call, one text, one search, one Internet hit away from moral jeopardy. Or that, absent serious misuse, a phone overall is still more a negative than a positive.

Not all kids will be controlled or misled by a smartphone. Unfortunately, the percentage who will is significant. And of those, many are good kids from good homes, where values and virtue are conscientiously taught.

Some kids on their own will keep the phone in balance. Some — okay, a few — won't even know where it is half the time. That said, follow an axiom of military strategy: Expect the best; prepare for the worst. Be always ready for what could happen, even if it never happens.

Re-Call

The cell phone has nestled into everyday life. The initial questions for a parent are: When do I allow one? And does it *have to be* a minicomputer?

You will hear voices from every direction — children, adults, society — to grant a phone well before it's time. Yours is the only voice that counts. You alone decide when, where, and how much phone.

No matter a child's age and moral maturity, there are no guarantees she will use a phone to her benefit. Therefore, vigilance is your indispensable ally. Robust rules and guardian technologies will dramatically lower the chance of bad use and raise the chance of good use.

6

Asocial Media

How would social media etiquette suit everyday life? To answer this, I'm conducting an experiment. Multiple times a day, I stroll through a store, striking up conversations with those who smile at me or just glance my way, whether I know them or not. I show them pictures of the caramel crusted donut I ate for breakfast, the parade of baby ducks that waddled in front of my car, my daughter's winning soccer goal, and my certificate for "employee of the week." To grab more attention, I hand them pictures of me in various poses and actions—walking on my treadmill, cleaning my bathroom sink, sitting on my couch eating pizza. I'm trying to get them to like me.

I eavesdrop on their conversations with others, too. I comment on their poetry, their favorite song lyrics, and their dog's new chew toy, all the while giving plenty of "thumbs up" signs of approval. And it's all working. Before the end of my first day, I already had four people following me—two police officers, a private eye, and a therapist.

Social Gains

The adage is: It's an ill wind that blows no good. In other words, something has to be really bad not to benefit anyone in any way. Social media isn't quite that bad: For its many downsides, it also has genuine upsides. Chief is its potential for fast and frequent connections.

Growing up, I had five pairs of aunts and uncles, two grandfathers, and a grandmother, all living within a six-mile radius. When I was four, my parents moved some seven miles away from my grandparents. Being Italian, I wondered if we were breaking some kind of law.

These days, families are scattered around the country or the world. Technology has built superhighways to make the miles irrelevant. It enables travel by cyberspace.

In college, my main tie to those back home was through letters — handwritten, in cursive. (Contrary to my children's belief, the pony express was no longer running.) Phones were around — the kind with cords and circles of numbers for dialing. But with long-distance charges only slightly lower that tuition, calls were few and short. By today's measure, communication was slow and costly.

Today's youth want and expect instant in-touch — Facetime, Skype, Snapchat, and so on. Anything handwritten might as well be hieroglyphic. How long before instant won't be fast enough?

This "right now" mentality, I confess, has shaped me, too. To heat my coffee in the morning, I'll set the microwave at sixty seconds. Around thirty seconds, I'm pacing like a panther, ordering the timer, "Come on, let's go! I haven't got all minute."

Technology, no matter how sophisticated and far-reaching, can never displace the personal. Still, it can complement it. It can draw closer those distant and those close closer still.

Two of our children are married, living in other states. Without cyber travel, our presence in their lives would be limited to a couple of visits per year, some photos, and a video or two. Nowadays, we can virtually see them and the grandkids whenever. Every so often, I still like to write a letter, so I web-search "Form letters for grandparents." They have several templates.

Asocial Media

Two of our children are in the military. They've been deployed to Afghanistan, Iraq, Africa, and Korea, as well as to bases around the country. When possible—or allowed—we make video contact. We know what is happening with them, and they with us. For instance, just last week, my son told me of walking twelve miles in triple-digit heat with a forty-pound rucksack. So I told him how I had to chase two toads out of the garage in my bare feet, at night. Not all that long ago, I would have shared my struggle in a letter arriving three weeks after the toads were long gone. Now I can let the kids know of my stress in real time.

When communication travels at the speed of light (186,200 miles per second!), distance doesn't exist. The virtue of social media resides in its capacity to forge ties and deepen love.

Couldn't the kids roam social media for the same benefit? Sure, and some do, but if that were the only, or even the main, draw of social media, the red flashing lights all around it wouldn't be so many or so bright.

Cell Mate

The numbers detailing the use, overuse, and misuse of smartphones parallel those for social media. That's no surprise, as the phone is its main artery. Time on the phone is now less talk and text, and more social media. Wandering its inexhaustible byways may be the most frequently shared human pursuit. About 3.1 billion people, or one of every three in the world, are users. Sixty-eight percent of Americans have a Facebook account. Three-fourths of them report checking it at least once a day, with half checking it several times.[15]

---

[15] John Gramlich, "10 Facts about Americans and Facebook," Pew Research Center, May 16, 2019, https://www.pewresearch.org/fact-tank/2019/05/16/facts-about-americans-and-facebook/.

Raising Upright Kids in an Upside-Down World

The average user spends upward of two hours a day immersed in social media, the most popular (for now) being Facebook, Instagram, Snapchat, and Twitter. More forums will keep rushing in. The math is sobering: Over a typical lifetime, the total time spent on these platforms is five-plus years. The teen's daily share is well above the adult's: Those who spend more than five hours per day double their risk of depression, girls more so than boys.

Last chapter urged a "no phone to bed" rule. Neither young nor older seem to like that rule. Seventy-one percent of people sleep with or within reach of their devices. Ten percent of teens check their phones more than ten times per night. How do they do that? Do they set its alarm to wake them on the hour? Do incoming calls and text chimes arouse them? Perhaps the scariest finding is that over 50 percent of drivers report checking social media when behind the wheel.[16]

"Those are group numbers. They include all kinds of families—good and bad. I don't think they apply to my child." Perhaps, but if grown-ups are vulnerable to the seduction of social media, kids with less maturity (not always) and more peer sway (not always) are even more vulnerable. They're not likely to moderate themselves. They need clear-eyed, resolute gatekeepers.

Self-Images

Do a web search: Children and self-esteem. The results have passed one hundred million—hard evidence that in only a few decades, self-esteem has vaulted from the classrooms of psychology professors

---

[16] "Pledge to Put Your #Phonedown During Distracted Driving Awareness Month," DriversEd.com, March 29, 2019, https://driversed. com/trending/pledge-put-your-phonedown-during-distracted-driving-awareness-month.

to the cultural consciousness. It has been elevated to the status of a virtue.

Academic success, achievements, healthy relationships, inner peace, smoother foreheads (okay, just a wish) — all sorts of personal pluses supposedly flow from a positive self-image. Likewise, emotional upheaval — self-doubt, anxiety, depression — is said to rise as self-esteem falls.

School bulletin boards are plastered with self-esteem mantras: "You can't like others if you don't like yourself." (Since when?) "I'm special." (If everybody is special, nobody is special.) "I'm a winner." (Participation trophies for all.)

"Self" is a high-profile word in the psychological lexicon — self-image, self-esteem, self-meaning, self-pursuit, self-help, self-autonomy. For some time, the theory has been that elevating one's self is critical to optimal living.

Reality is the final judge of every "sounds good" notion of well-being. The self-esteem juggernaut has been tested and found wanting. Most of its claims have unraveled with closer scrutiny. Not to put down self-esteem, but it actually isn't related to overall well-being. It is better viewed as a by-product of being loved unconditionally, along with a solid sense of one's strengths and weaknesses.

Pursuing self-esteem for its own sake can lead to some negative "selfs" — self-centeredness, self-absorption, self-promotion.

Teresa Tomeo, a national radio host, has authored a book called *Me, My Selfie, and I*. It speaks to the "selfie" frenzy — endless pictures of me here, there, and everywhere with him, her, and them. It's a "look at me" temptation to faux self-esteem. In the extreme, it tempts young people toward the ultimate selfie shot, one whose backdrop risks their safety, or their very lives.

Not all that long ago, self-photos took two people. That is, somebody else had to take my picture. And asking him to devote forty-five minutes of his time while I pose repeatedly across changing backdrops, well, that just might strain our friendship. No longer. I don't need a photographer. I can do it myself and scatter my portfolio all over the nearby universe. Talk about inflated self-images.

Daily Christmas Letters

Everyone who gets Christmas cards gets a few "family letters" tucked inside — yearly updates about a family's doings since last Christmas. Some are unpretentious greetings, and some are not-so-subtle brag recitals.

> My daughter, Bliss, turned eleven and just completed her tenth year of ballet, gymnastics, competitive powerlifting, and Greco-Roman language scholarship. She's been busy gearing up for her Olympic tryouts in 2020. Hopefully she'll be able to juggle that with her pending nomination as Junior Ambassador to NATO.
>
> Her brother Noble was surprised on his sixth birthday with calls from the pope, the president, and two of the Beatles. His birthday party had to be cut short because we all had to leave for a week-long cruise honoring him for winning our state's 2018 First Grader of the Year Award.
>
> My husband, Forbes, has been named regional sales manager for the Northeast section of the Milky Way, and I keep active, volunteering at the nursing home ten to twelve hours a day, knitting shawls for the residents, and teaching them sign language.
>
> The real go-getter of the family, though, is big brother Sterling, who just last week ..."

Unbridled social media can be a daily Christmas letter on steroids. It can feed the appetite to preen, to chronicle every accomplishment, no matter how minor. It enables one to send a parade of words and images in front of anyone, interested or not.

Admission: I set up a Facebook page a few years ago. A colleague convinced me it could help others. For years, I resisted having a social media presence because I didn't trust myself. Should others want my advice, I feared I'd start believing they'd likewise want to hear about my day. Behind the page lurks the temptation to broadcast, "Look at me. Am I cool or what?" Never underestimate the power of the post for self-promotion.

Is your youngster gorging on social media? Impose a fast. The benefits will show up within days. One study offered participants money to shun social media for one month. That they had to pay people to participate says a lot. Those who kept the fast reported more life contentment and resurgent interest in formerly abandoned activities. What would your child charge to stay media free for a month? How about for an hour?

Not to keep dialing the same number, but flip phones can't access social media. Neither can smartphones with Web controls. In case you're interested, some ideas are on my Facebook Page, along with a picture of me cliff driving (photoshopped).

Virtual Stickers

Elementary schools methodically systematize targeted behavioral interventions, applying positive reinforcement procedures, augmented by a variable ratio schedule. All right, they give stickers for good behavior. The teachers want, to use trendy value-neutral language, "appropriate" conduct, and the kids want stickers. As the motivational speakers would say: It's a win-win.

Sticker systems work better with little kids. Or so it was once thought.

Raising Upright Kids in an Upside-Down World

Social media is a high-tech sticker system, dispensing rewards to all ages, for any kind of behavior, good or bad. Nothing yet from the minds of psychologists is better at feeding the human longing for rewards than social media. And while Mrs. Gradehard can run out of stickers, Instagram never will.

Stickers suffer a limitation: Kids get bored with them. "I already have eight Spiderman ones. These are all the same."

Social media suffers from a similar limitation. What once supplied a potent feel-good—playing to one's initial audience—over time loses luster. A bigger audience is needed to achieve the same rush. Numbers come to equal social status. Comparing oneself with those with hundreds or thousands, even millions, of followers can lead to feeling insignificant. It can result in a self-image graded on a harsh curve.

Also at work is something called a "variable ratio reinforcement schedule." Stripped of its academic language, it simply means "rewards at random." All slot machines work on a variable ratio schedule. Because a player can't know when he might win, to win a few times he needs to play many times. Thus, he will yank levers and push buttons until tendonitis sets in. Pigeons, pecking for seeds dispensed on a variable ratio schedule, will drop from exhaustion.

Anyone who plays the social media slots quickly finds that winning is erratic. Some posts evoke barely a nod, others a chorus of cheers, and rare ones go viral. In social media parlance, to go viral is akin to winning a lottery. How ironic that "viral," once connoting a threat to health, now means cyber celebrity. Technology doesn't only change life; it changes language.

Behavior theory predicts: To get more of some behavior, reward it at random. When playing a social slot machine, keep cranking. Put up more posts. Raise the odds of scoring, socially and emotionally. The formula is perfect for breeding obsessive conduct. Pigeons anyone?

The Mob

Psychologists are intrigued by mobs. How does a mob move collectively? What fans its energy? What makes it go violent? Why would an otherwise passive person get aggressive in a mob?

"Diffusion of responsibility" is one answer: No individual is responsible for the mob's actions. It behaves as one. The mob is not a medley of unique personalities. It is a solo personality.

A second answer: Anonymity. Faces in the crowd blur into one face. No one stands out unless he seeks to. Anonymity protects.

Road rage is mob psychology miniaturized. Recently I drove up to an unfamiliar, tricky intersection. Thinking I had to yield, I slowed down. When I saw no stop or yield sign, I began to accelerate. Too late. Immediately, the car behind me blared its horn, along with an easy-to-read lip message.

At the next intersection, the driver pulled next to me. She looked to be in her mid-seventies and was still fuming at my driving lapse. Were we in line at a fast-food counter and I had delayed her somehow, I doubt she'd be so free to assail me. Much too up close and personal for that. In her car, from thirty feet away, she was far more brazen.

It's a social law: The more anonymity, the less restraint. This is particularly so when the behavior is mean—which makes social media a perfect venue for letting loose all manner of words and images one would stifle in other circumstances.

Schools are hyperalert to bullying, offering all kinds of instruction to counter it. Where they can see it, they can intervene. Where they can't see, or can't identify someone, they are rendered helpless.

Young people, of course, have incomplete self-restraint. Then again, who has complete self-restraint, no matter the age? Provide an untraceable outlet for what is percolating inside, and the urge to go public can overwhelm.

Raising Upright Kids in an Upside-Down World

The Big Interview

Sean and Sarah graduated from the same college in the same year with the same degree. They had been searching for a career in their field. Finally, an employer who, on paper, looked exactly like what they had been seeking, contacted them.

Both presented themselves as knowledgeable and personable, becoming the two finalists. The interviewers were evenly divided about who should get the position.

Two days later, Sarah got hired. Who—or what—broke the tie? Sean's social media. It revealed a side of him quite unlike his interview persona. He was caught by a social media by-product: Employers are checking into cyber accounts to select the best candidates.

Nowhere is background more scrutinized than in law enforcement, security, and government agencies. Further, even if a young adult has outgrown questionable or offensive posts, whatever is lingering from his past may be enough to delete some of his career options.

Not much lasts forever, unless it's somewhere on social media. Were Perpetua to expunge all youthful foolishness, others' accounts may still store some of it. Kids don't naturally look too far into the future. Parents have to look for them.

Protecting kids from misused social media is far from easy. Parents can't always track what is happening in their child's online world. Technology is a youngster's second language. Most parents still need a translator.

Repeat to your kids: Never, ever go public with anything that could one day boomerang on you or someone you care about. You can't know how what you put into the public now will hurt you privately someday. How important is a good job anyway?

The good news: A sharp-eyed parent, looking over a child's shoulder, has a better chance of detecting ugly stuff, going or coming. Eventually it will materialize. A pattern doesn't stay hidden forever. And a privilege abused is a privilege gone. Perhaps for some time.

All Jekyll, No Hyde

Strong-willed, challenging, mind of his own, eight going on eighteen, a difficult child. (Is "difficult child" redundant?) Standard descriptions of children these days. "What does his teacher say?" I query. "I don't understand it. She says he's a delight. He gives her no trouble at all."

Hearing these accolades, a parent will stare stupefied at the teacher and, pulling out a wallet photo, will ask, "Is this the child? Brown-haired boy with a gap in his teeth? Who are you? What school is this?"

The wife of a grouch meets a woman who regales her, "Your husband is so nice to work with. He's such a gentleman, always complimenting everybody." Wife has to choke back, "What's his last name? I think you may be confusing me with someone else."

How does one reconcile the personality of home child with school child, or grouch spouse with employee of the year? Simple: They don't need to be reconciled. It is part of being human: Our conduct is highly influenced by where we are, whom we're with, and how much we want and need their approval. The saying is: We are not so much moved by what others think of us, but by what we think they think of us.

Social media provides the audience for us to think about what they think of us. The urge to look good, not just in pictures but in words, feelings, and opinions, can be irresistible. As the country song notes, "I'm a whole lot cooler online."

Pictures aren't the only things that can be photoshopped. Personalities can be, too — swimmingly happy, perpetually entertained, forever friendly, deep in romance. Social media is an open forum to fashion a one-sided image of who we are.

Again, this can easily induce ongoing comparisons. It sure does look as if all these other people are leading upbeat, pleasure-driven lives. I may look like that, too, but I know the reality isn't so. I feel as if I'm falling short. Is something wrong with me?

In Robert Louis Stevenson's *Dr. Jekyll and Mr. Hyde*, Dr. Jekyll brews a potion that splits his personality into a good side (Dr. Jekyll) and a bad side (Mr. Hyde). Jekyll is an upstanding, well-respected pillar of society. Hyde is a brutish, nasty social misfit. For many, Dr. Jekyll is their social media side. There's nothing wrong with wanting to look good for others, but when it devolves to a need, one will feel obliged to fabricate more and more of life. In the online image competition, it is unavoidable: There will be winners and losers.

It's Here

The forces and fears that can distort a parent's good judgment are pervasive and potent. One, pressure—from children, parents, society. Two, assorted what-ifs—What if I provoke resentment, rebellion, isolation, alienation? Three, accusations—controlling, constricting, overprotective, out of touch.

A fourth reason moves parents to grant freedoms prematurely. It has little to do with outside pressure. It is not psychologically unsettling. It is basic: Because it's here.

What's here? Social media. It is cultural oxygen. Teens inhale it deeply. Anything that gains "new reality" status comes to be unquestionably accepted. Whatever its downsides, whatever its risks, whether on balance it is good or bad: It is not scrutinized. It is present life. It is just here.

"Why are you permitting so much social media in your adolescent's life?" I ask parents. They look at me as if I just asked, "Why do you have a car?" Their answers, in so many words are, "Isn't that just what kids do?" Even if they are queasy about "what kids do," they don't act on their instincts. They don't give themselves the authority to challenge something so apparently ubiquitous to youth.

"Just here" does not imply "just good." Or even "just okay." Whatever is here needs to be questioned. Is it obsessive? Is it altering my child's personality? Is it sabotaging healthier priorities? Is it usurping time from better pursuits?

Re-Post

Social—meaning people. Media—meaning communication. The beauty of social media lies in bringing people together—from near or far. The ugliness of social media lies in bringing people together, some of whom should never be allowed within a continent of a child's world.

You can cavort as you wish throughout the social media landscape. You are a grown-up. You make your own decisions—good or bad, smart or foolish.

Few kids are grown up. Left alone, they can make more bad decisions than good, more dumb than smart. Parents are called to adjust the ratio of smart to dumb in their child's favor.

It's basic: More social media, less personal growth. Few things can stunt the growth of a child's character more than unlimited access to social media.

It is a counterfeit of deeper relationships. It feeds the self: self-absorption, self-seeking, self-promotion. And it provokes self-critical comparisons.

Social media is a staple of the culture. Its allure is more acute among the young. Social media will not govern itself. You must govern its presence and pull. Or else it will govern your child.

7

Computer Savvy

Recently I took my three-year-old computer for service. The young technician eyed it, mystified, as though I had just carried in an abacus. His demeanor said, "Where did you get this? Where's the crank to start it?" From my car to his counter, I went from avant-garde to aboriginal.

In first-year engineering, for a course in computer programming, I hauled boxes of "punch cards" to the building that housed the computer — an imposing, wall-spanning machine that wasn't a whole lot more than a sophisticated calculator. I knew then that I could never afford a house large enough to hold a computer. Wrong.

A few decades after graduating, I sat a computer, smaller than our television, under a desk in our family room. My eight-year-old son fluttered toward it instantly. It was a bright light, and he was a moth. Years later, he graduated with a technology degree, unlike his father.

Our permanent resident had skills exponentially beyond its mammoth forerunner. Chief among them was transporting its operator to anywhere and anybody, though many of these places and people weren't safe for a little boy. We had to learn fast how to erect some "road closed" signs.

Size Safety

A classic song goes: *Anything you can do, I can do better.* Technology could sing a similar song: *Anything you can do, I can do smaller.*

Anything a computer can do, a smartphone can pretty much do, at half the size of those primitive punch cards. How soon before handheld is oversized? What's on the horizon? Fingernail screens? On pinky fingers?

The guidelines for smarter phone handling almost all apply to the computer as well. Nonetheless, the computer does afford some unique safeguards.

Size. Unlike a phone, a computer can't follow a child everywhere. A pocket or purse can't hold or hide one—not easily anyway. Though shrinking rapidly, computers are still larger than phones, and being easier to see makes them easier to oversee.

Optimum Staging

Realtors recommend "staging" a house for a quicker sale. Meaning, make it look warm and homey. Basic to good staging is furniture placement. Where does the furniture sit? Basic to good supervision is computer placement. Where does the computer sit?

Bedrooms are bad rooms for computers. They are out of sight and thereby out of mind. Likewise, so are finished basements. It's a law of human nature: One is more likely to act badly when no one else is watching, or when no one else is close enough to watch.

A vigilant parent isn't misled by false notions about a child's privacy. At any time, she is willing to peer over her child's shoulder. That's not possible when walls block her eyes.

Some families give the computer its own room—a testament to its lofty status. Growing up, I never had my own room. I'm not sure what that says about my status.

Whether a room helps or hinders oversight depends on lines of sight—what you can see from where. Can you position mirrors? You know, the kind that let you look around corners.

Our first computer was strategically parked in the family room, making it observable from much of the kitchen, most of the living room, and all of the family room. From just about any place on our first floor, we could monitor the monitor.

The kitchen is another good computer room. In most homes, the kitchen is at the heart of the action. It is where people eat, sit, and pass through all day long. For highest visibility, not much beats the kitchen. It affords optimum staging.

Should Parker not agree with your staging, he is telling you: "I don't want your eyes on me." Confirmation that you're wise to keep the computer in sight.

Glitchy Vigilance

Parents are rocked after discovering their child's foray into the seamier corners of the Web. Yet many had never set up safeguards. One survey found that while two-thirds of middle schoolers, half of ten- to twelve-year-olds, and a quarter of preschoolers regularly spent heavy time on the computer, less than half of their parents locked down the Internet in any way. Only 38 percent did so for the phone. More stunning, just 40 percent of parents monitored their four-year-olds' devices.[17] Yikes!

Yet, four-fifths of these parents worried that they weren't able to keep close watch on their kids' online whereabouts. Why didn't their worry translate into more oversight?

---

[17] "Teen Internet Use and Parental Controls," *The Mac Security Blog*, Intego, January 6, 2017, https://www.intego.com/mac-security-blog/infographic-teen-internet-use-and-parental-controls/.

Raising Upright Kids in an Upside-Down World

"I never thought he'd do something like that." So say parents after a child's phone misuse. Indeed, he may be a good kid, but he's still a kid, with curiosity, naïveté, and a young conscience. He wouldn't be left unsupervised at age eight, ten, or twelve to romp at a playground two miles from home, but he's romping unsupervised all over a global playground.

As a parent, early on I was intimidated—not so much by my children, but by the computer. Its powers were multiplying far faster than my rudimentary understanding of its powers. Hearing from others who had been Web-smacked told me I had better educate myself. Or, more precisely, I had better find someone who was better educated than I. So I turned to the tech pros. I wasn't real smart about how to discipline the Web. They were.

Fatigue can creep in. The attitude, as with social media, is, "It's everywhere. It's part of childhood now. It's kids' second language." Because the Web is everywhere, it's all the more imperative that a parent doesn't just live with it but acts resolutely to rule it.

Parent Protection Plan

We have one child still living at home. I tease her, "After you move on, Mom and I are getting into a Parent Protection Plan. Our identities will be altered, and we will be relocated to a remote cabin in Northern Canada." We will live in seclusion, at least until the kids locate us via Google Maps.

Every kid needs a different kind of Parent Protection Plan. The steps are simple. One: Keep the computer in plain sight. Two: Password protect it. This renders the computer comatose until you personally sign in to wake it. A password defends against post-midnight log-ins. Basic advice: Nothing obvious—your address, birth date, dog's name, "Open Sesame!" I was tempted to make my password "incorrect," so, should I forget and type in the wrong one, my computer will instruct me, "Your password is incorrect." Thank you.

Three: Set parental controls. These block entry to any and all sites or apps of your choosing. They also will report where your child has been or tried to go. They allow you to set specific times of operation, say 4:00 to 5:00 p.m., or 7:30 to 8:30 p.m., or 5:01 to 5:03 p.m. The computer automatically denies access after the expiration time.

The options for Internet safety parallel those for smartphones, with more emerging even as you read this. The Internet itself will help you find good ones.

Libraries, unfortunately, don't always match a parent's watchfulness. Does your library protect its young users? If minimally or not at all, you may have to supervise your kids' visits. Can you read a book right behind Webster as he sits at the computer terminal?

Many schools provide the kids devices to use for schoolwork. Your best protection is to "pair" your child's device to one or all of yours. Whatever happens on your child's device will instantly show up on yours. You'll see everything. Don't know how to pair? I can send you my fourth-grade nephew's number. He knows how. Keep trying, though. He gets lots of calls from parents.

The Web is a wondrous world. Tragically, there are those—proliferating wildly every day—who corrupt it to prey, seduce, and misguide. And those most targeted and most vulnerable are children.

The very best controls and filters are not foolproof. The most tenacious Web sentinel remains a parent. Nothing substitutes for your watchful eyes motivated by love.

Vidimeds

More size means less secrecy. More size also means more appeal. While Oscar can entertain himself with a phone's three-inch images, a computer projects bigger and better images. A TV, even more so. The larger the image, the more engaging. This explains why televisions are stretching toward the dimensions of movie screens.

"He's really into video games. He fixates on them, always pushing for the next chance to play." What is it about video games that so thoroughly steals kids' time and attention, particularly boys'? Simple answer: They're designed to do so.

The formula is foolproof: Begin with extremely talented game creators. Add lifelike graphics and hyperpaced action. Reward performance instantly. Build in social competition — others gaming along. In place are all the elements needed to seize someone — child or adult — by the senses. By comparison, real life looks slow and dull. School and church? Lame.

A common scenario: Around age five, Mario begins his game pleas. Other kids have them; TV hustles them; they're supercool; and he doesn't yet have even one. He's fast falling behind all his cousins. It's so unfair. His relentless appeals finally move Mom and Dad to purchase a few of the more benign games. "We'll get mostly educational ones," they initially reason.

For a little while, Mario is content with what he gets. But as is their way, the games enthrall, and Mario presses harder for more time and more intense action. Whether this progression (regression?) spans three months or three years, it's a given: The more Mario plays, the more he will not just want but crave to play. Curbing his time is not acceptable to him. There will be pushback.

A late-night television host challenged parents: "While your child is playing [a hot new video game], without words or warning, shut down the screen." So some intrepid parents did. The kids' reactions? In a word, hysterical — screaming, limbs flailing, cursing. A few kids swung at parents. The spectacles made a toddler's meltdown look like Victorian etiquette. All the while, the studio audience found it uproarious.

Of course, the show's producers aired the most raving displays. Still, if a picture is worth a thousand words, these pictures were worth ten thousand. The kids all looked to be between ages eight and thirteen. Likely they had been living in video land for years. No one game on its own, no matter how mesmerizing, could provoke such wild-eyed resistance.

Every player was a boy. No surprise, as any parent of both sexes sees up close and research confirms: Male and female brains are wired differently. Boys are more drawn to images, action, and risks—the very predispositions stoked by video games.

The chief gamers are not solely adolescent boys, destined to outgrow their obsession as adulthood beckons. They include men ages eighteen to thirty, much to the ongoing frustration of their girlfriends and wives. Gaming is preempting their relationships, family life, or dad-kid time.

One wife spoke for many when she pleaded: Moms, if you want another reason for controlling your sons' game mania, think of the women in their futures. Will they have to endure a grown-up adolescent still consuming hours of games each week or even each day? Will they feel neglected and less appealing than the virtual world?

I echo her words. Too much gaming won't affect just your family. It could someday affect his family.

Plea Bargain

Fast forward several years. Mario has mastered the art of playing the game to get a game. He's learned where and how to score points. When the opportunity presents itself, he jumps to make his case. By chance, I was in the next aisle over, so I heard Mario and his mother spar.

Raising Upright Kids in an Upside-Down World

MARIO: Look, Mom. Mom, look. Here's that video game I was telling you about. The one I keep seeing on TV. It's really neat, and you said I could get it.

MOM: No, I never said you could get it. I said, "We'll see."

DR. RAY: In parent talk, "We'll see" doesn't mean "Yes." It means, "I'm putting off my decision." In kid talk, "We'll see" signals that a "Yes" is only a matter of time and, if need be, some well-targeted nagging. Unless one really does mean "Yes," it's smart to avoid the phrase "We'll see." It just asks for a protracted pushing for permission.

MOM: You've got plenty of video games. Grandma just bought you two more for your birthday. Besides, I don't know anything about that game.

MARIO: Yes, you do. I told you before. It's the one where you have to drive a car through all kinds of traffic jams and see how fast you can get someplace. It's really cool.

MOM: It doesn't sound so cool to me. It sounds like it teaches you to be reckless. Anyway, forget it for this time around.

DR. RAY: "This time around"? Is this a variant of "We'll see"? Is Mom willingly asking for more badgering next time around? And the next? In an effort to close the exchange for now, she's leaving it open down the road.

MARIO: Mom, the ones Grandma got me are for little kids. All they do is show you some math facts I already know.

MOM: That's good. It won't hurt you to get more practice. You don't know your math facts as well as you think.

MARIO: Aw, come on, Mom. Just this one game. Then I won't ask for any more for a long time.

DR. RAY: The next step after an appeal to a parent's "reason" has failed is an appeal to emotions. If that lands on a stony heart, execute the fatigue factor. Wear the big person down.

MARIO: Mom, I already played it once at Chevy's house. His dad even played it with us. Please, Mom. It's my favorite of all the games. Please, huh?

MOM: No, Mario. Now, that's it. I'm not going to argue about this anymore.

MARIO: Mom, look. See, it says, "For ages eight and up." I'm ten. It's even got three stars on it because School Mountain says it's a good one for coordination.

DR. RAY: Mom may be ready to quit arguing, but Mario isn't. He's keeping his foot to the accelerator. She'll have to be the one to slam on the brakes. Notice, too, the shaping power of "You've got to have this" advertising aimed at kids. The only way to limit its pull is to limit its presence. Slow down on the TV. Mario won't be so acutely aware of the latest must-have goodie. And he won't be so driven to have it.

MOM: You can keep nagging all you want, Mario, but it's not going to work. I am not buying *Car Maniac* for you.

DR. RAY: As the hectoring continues, Mom strives to stay resolute in the face of more words and higher volume, not to mention the looks of nearby shoppers. Sometimes offering an adolescent forty dollars per hour plus benefits to babysit while you shop alone is a small price to pay.

MARIO: If I can't have it this time, maybe next time? When we get home, I'll show you what games we can get rid of because I don't play them anymore. We can give them to kids who don't have any. I'll give away five for this one, okay?

MOM: We'll see.[18]

When it comes to the newest video games, a parent has to be very clear in her answer. Anything less leaves too much wiggle room.

---

[18] Adapted from Guarendi, *Winning the Discipline Debates*.

Raising Upright Kids in an Upside-Down World

Power Down

Major just can't get his fill of *Power Combat*. He badgers for extra time, argues against quitting, and stretches every session. There's more combat at home than on the screen.

Some experts advise: Avoid a "power struggle." Find a compromise. Give a little ground, and Major will do likewise. Sounds workable on paper. Real kids eat paper.

What if you think Major's attachment is already too great? To find middle ground, will you have to grant more time? If you believe your conditions are reasonable, why alter them because Major finds them unreasonable?

Video games hurtle on fast-forward, yanking kids along with them. You have the power to slow or stop them whenever you see fit, or whenever you see a fit.

Video Vile-ence

Over 90 percent of kids ages twelve to seventeen play video games. More than half of the top-selling games contain extremely graphic violence. The question is as old as moving images themselves: Does watching on-screen violence lead to off-screen violence? From movies to television to video games, the movement toward more realistic portrayals of vile human conduct continues, lending more urgency to answering the question.

To say that the subject has been scrutinized forward, backward, and sideways by professionals would be a major understatement. And the consensus moves in one direction: The more companionship with violent media, the more risk of aggressive behavior. Ninety-eight percent of pediatricians agree with that conclusion, as do 80 percent of researchers.[19] Six medical associations, includ-

[19] Brad J. Bushman, Mario Gollwitzer, and Carlos Cruz, "There Is Broad Consensus: Media Researchers Agree That Violent Media

ing the American Medical Association (AMA) and the American Psychological Association, agree that there is a connection between media violence and aggressive behavior in some children.

Case closed, right? Not quite. Like so much human conduct, it is often simplistic to say, "A causes B." More likely, "A causes B, depending on C, D, E, F . . ."

Note that the AMA said "in some children." Which children? Those raised in unstable, turbulent environments? Those on a heavy regimen of vicious videos? Those whose temperament is more inclined to aggression? Those with little or no adult supervision?

All of these can contribute, but probably none describe your family. So the games shouldn't cause that much trouble, right? Maybe not. But to raise a great kid, as always the question is not "Will this do harm?" but "Will this do good?"

Is there benefit to watching people, animals, even bad-guy zombies getting gunned down, vaporized, blown up? If you think not, then why allow the game? Because it's not as rough as what else is out there? Because it's available? Because Wyatt wants it? Because Grandma bought it for him? Because he can "socialize" through it with others? Are there not better things he can do with his time?

What about desensitization? Does immersion in virtual violence numb one's reluctance to commit real violence? Does it override the innate hesitancy to hurt another? Again, researchers debate that, but some evidence does point toward that possibility.

In fact, the military has experimented with using "point and shoot" video games to desensitize recruits to firing actual weapons in combat. Back in 2002, the army had already released a shooter game to ready recruits to shoot for real. If it's uncertain whether

Increase Aggression in Children, and Pediatricians and Parents Concur," *Psychology of Popular Media Culture* 4, no. 3 (2015): 200–214.

or how much savage games might actually desensitize, wouldn't it be better to err on the safe side?

My five sons had screen games: baseball, football, basketball, car races. We considered them kid-friendly fun and gave them a controlled place in our home. Had the boys progressively pestered us, or had the games become the focus of a fracas, well, we had a real live backyard for kickball and football.

Boo-Tube

A distraught father contacted me after his five-year-old son had emotionally collided with "YouTube Kids." While the little guy was enjoying a charming kid story, a witch-like woman burst in, urging the kids to get up and hurt their parents. Fortunately, the little guy didn't fully understand her, but she scared him, and he ran to find his father. By the time Dad got to the screen, the intruder had vanished.

YouTube gives new meaning to "worldwide network." It boasts millions of actors, directors, and producers, any of whom can be called up with a flick of a finger. Anything—and I mean anything—can be seen on it. Much of it is informative, entertaining, or uplifting. Much of it is perverse and evil.

Neither dad nor son remotely anticipated what interrupted their regularly scheduled programming. The little guy was naïve, as are most five-year-olds. Dad was naïve, as are many parents struggling to keep pace with galloping technology and its manifold corruptions.

In an ideal world, every modern marvel would be used only for good. Such is not the world we live in. Therefore, a parent must keep a child's world ideal for as long as possible.

"There is good stuff on YouTube." No argument about that. Can you ensure that's all Nielson will see or seek? Plenty of people occupying (and running) YouTube don't give one moral whit about your child or anybody's child.

A public service message: No little kid should be anywhere near YouTube. "Little" here is defined as under six feet, two inches. That means five-year-olds, nine-year-olds, thirteen-year-olds. If Emmy is never primed for YouTube viewing, she won't know what she's missing. And much of what she's missing, she should be missing.

More Screen, Less Commitment

"He pushed hard for drum lessons. Two months into them, he's fighting me to practice." "She wanted to run cross-country. Now she says she wants to quit." "He was all enthused about learning martial arts. His enthusiasm left as fast as it came."

Commitment—a cardinal quality for a well-lived life. Parents work hard to instill it but often find it harder than they expected. "Why is he so quick to lose interest? Why can't she seem to stay with something? How long do I try to force a commitment? How much do I push?"

When I was twelve, my parents purchased an organ for my younger sister. "I want to play, too," I nagged. Not all that many lessons later, just as my musical fervor was going flat, my teacher told my father, "He has natural talent." (Who asked her? The lady talked too much.)

That convinced Pop. (The man listened too much.) His son would take more lessons. As time ticked onward, I was sure my dad and teacher were both singing the wrong tune. My well-practiced argument: "It's not like I'm going to be a professional or something."

Once past my peak opposition, and as I was getting more musically sharp despite my worst efforts, this keyboard thing started to sound tolerable. Some years later, I turned "professional or something" and performed in restaurants through my college years —graduating debt-free and having gained a lifelong skill.

How much more resistance would I have given my parents if other, more-entertaining virtual alternatives had been calling to me? As it was, football, TV, and sleep competed with practicing. Throw video options into the mix, and the score would have been: Games—Lots; Organ—0.

The relationship is inverse: The more commitment to the screen, the less to other pursuits. The games rely on second-by-second gratification. Gaining competence in most life skills takes time and perseverance. The rewards unfold gradually. Granted, screen time may not be the sole player in a child's flagging interest in "more boring stuff." Nonetheless, when too available, it can be a major factor.

Commitment Rules

- Set the timetable. How long must a child persevere in an activity that he claimed he wanted before quitting is permitted?
- A season started is a season finished. Obligation is not only to the sport, but more so to one's teammates.
- All practice sessions take priority over privileges, especially screen privileges. Privileges don't begin until practice is complete.
- Should Ludwig make his practicing more taxing on you than on him, replace practice time with work time, at a ratio of two to one. For example, one hour of chores replaces a half hour of practice. It shouldn't be too long before Ludwig chooses to practice.
- Any commitment renounced early leads also to suspended video activity. If Cosmo wants to drop astronomy club two moons early, no games for the next two months.

- Rich reimburses you for the money you fronted for any prematurely dropped activity.

The games can foster a strong sense of commitment — to them.

Re-Boot

The computer and the smartphone are relatives. The computer is the older, bigger brother. It has lived in the family longer.

The old warning: Big Brother is watching you. The new warning: You'd better watch Big Brother. A computer needs the same parental controls as a smartphone. Because it's bigger and less private than a phone, it is also easier to supervise. Place it in your house where you can easily monitor it. Lines of sight makes for good oversight.

Bigger does have its downside. Games rely on screen size for maximum effect. They capture the senses with furious, split-second action. The larger the images, the stronger the attraction.

Video games can become a drug. The only way to blunt their effects is to regulate when, what, and how much the dose. Then again, total withdrawal is an option. With YouTube, too.

8

TV or Not TV

My earliest recollections of gazing at a TV screen come from around age three. Contrary to my kids' belief, television had already been invented, shortly after the wheel. And it didn't take long for TV to grab a primetime place in my childhood.

My TV menu offered three channels, all local affiliates, and all aired in black and white. If you wanted color, you could tape tinted cellophane over the screen. It didn't fool anybody.

Our television had a remote: me. "Ray, see what's on the other channel." "It's too loud, Ray, can you turn it down a little?" To this day, I regale my children, "I had to get up and walk across six feet of shag carpet several times a night. That's the way it was when I was a boy."

What will our kids tell their kids? "Five hundred fifty channels—that's all we had when we were kids. The screen barely covered half the wall—in only two dimensions. Our five remotes all had their power buttons at the top. You had to stretch your finger up there. That probably explains the arthritis in my thumb."

For the most part, my parents weren't nervous about what the TV said and showed to me. Whatever the program or its commercials, they didn't insult or assault my parents' core beliefs. Their values and the TV's were on the same wavelength. At least in those early years.

Screen Browsing

One large-scale survey reported that average daily viewing among young people ages eighteen to twenty-four has dropped by roughly ninety minutes since 2012.[20] In the twelve-to-seventeen age group, TV time is down by more than half, to just under ten hours per week.[21] (Recall that 2012 was the year smartphone ownership surpassed 50 percent.) Across surveys the trend is consistent: TV time among youth is dropping.

That's the good news. The bad news: *Overall* screen time has not fallen. It's just shifted. The 50 percent drop in kids' viewing habits has migrated to other screens—computer, phone, social media.

No longer the unchallenged molder of modern morality, TV still remains a potent pusher of "enlightened" attitudes and values. Its persuasive power is magnified by its appeal. It is unrestrained entertainment. And it uses "charm" to make bad look good, wrong look right, immoral look cool.

Brutal World

The TV world is a fun-house mirror of the real world. Most people seek to live peaceful, stable lives. Television, by contrast, beams upheaval and ugliness. For instance, while few have ever actually

---

[20] "The State of Traditional TV: Updated with Q2 2017 Data," Marketing Charts, December 26, 2018, https://www.marketingcharts. com/television-24817.

[21] "The State of Traditional TV: Updated with Q3 2018 Data," Marketing Charts, April 3, 2019, https://www.marketingcharts.com/ featured-105414.

witnessed a violent crime, by the time a child leaves elementary school, estimates are that he has watched roughly eight thousand on-screen murders, with 100,000-plus acts of violence. After combing the studies, the surgeon general reported (1993) that heavy exposure to media violence is connected to "violent, aggressive and hostile behavior." And in 1993, TV was still a little more morally congenial.

As with video games, the question follows: Who is most affected, and how much? Again, that's hard to know or predict. While good parenting can go a long way to counter bad viewing, if absorbing toxic TV has any risks for any child, why let it seep in?

An exasperating misbehavior for parents is "sibling quibbling," the everyday (every hour?) bickering that erupts among brothers and sisters. Without closed-circuit cameras in every room, a parent can get disoriented trying to get to the bottom of who said what to whom, when, where, and how much. At times, words escalate to force. Somebody gets pushed, pinched, kicked, hit.

Would too much ugly TV incite a child's reflexive resort to the physical? Does it play a part in provoking more sibling assaults? The link may be unclear. That doesn't mean there's no link.

"Not every child is going to be influenced by everything he sees." Certainly. A thing doesn't have to affect everybody equally, though, for it to have some effect on many. Every advertisement for the coolest car doesn't move every viewer to buy the car. But every viewer will know the car is available.

Anytime, Anyone Sex

More so even than violence, television traffics in sex. The message is: If it feels good—or even if it doesn't—do it. In an analysis of prime-time TV shows, more than three-fourths presented sexual content, with less than 15 percent presenting anything about responsibility, abstinence, pregnancy, or sexually transmitted diseases. And morality? It's the one taboo topic.

The studies are of one voice: The medium has inexhaustible energy to shape teens' approach to love and sex.[22] If they see it, they'll believe it. Perhaps not always—but enough.

Other studies make it clear that it isn't just images, but also talk, jokes, and innuendos that nudge teens to premature sexual activity, along with thinking that premarital and extramarital relations with multiple partners is just fine.[23]

In short, the relentlessly libertine portrayal of TV sex dramatically misshapes how the young think and behave.

Parallel Universe

"Television doesn't influence people. It merely reflects society as it is." So goes the argument, reiterated mostly by media moguls. If so, why would programs charge tens of thousands of dollars—in some cases, tens of millions—for a thirty- or sixty-second ad that is just a forgettable eye rest from the main event? Are they claiming that a thirty-minute presentation doesn't persuade but a thirty-second one does? That might be so only if one falls asleep during the show but wakes for the commercials. If television doesn't sway viewers, then the TV people are cheating the ad people.

On any Sunday, about 40 percent of the U.S. population is in church or synagogue. What percentage of people are shown attending church on TV? Nearly the same percentage, around

---

[22] Jane D. Brown and V. C. Strasburger, "From Calvin Klein to Paris Hilton and MySpace: Adolescents, Sex, and the Media," *Adolescent Medicine: State of the Art Reviews* 18, no. 3 (2007): 484–507.

[23] Jane D. Brown, Kim Walsh Childers, and Cynthia S. Waszak, "Television and Adolescent Sexuality," *Journal of Adolescent Health Care* 11, no. 1 (1990): 62–70.

40, pray before meals. Though a few older programs portray the practice, almost none do now. On TV, 40 percent of murders are committed by businessmen. In reality, less than one-half of 1 percent are. Adults drink water seven times as much as they drink alcohol. Television reverses that ratio.[24] To borrow a storyline from Superman comics, TV is Bizarro World, where everything is the opposite of earth.

A news tease boasted, "When we get back, we'll talk to the sixth graders at [the school] to get the real scoop." Huh? Twelve-years-olds are the most reliable reporters? My own twelve-year-olds thought they were. I didn't.

You don't need to be a psychologist to know that everybody sees the world through his own lens, sometimes a clouded or warped one. Kids, due to their immaturity and inexperience, are even more prone to misread reality. Who, besides news reporters, would think juveniles the most insightful and unbiased sources?

Television would. Programs consistently parade kids and adolescents in the lead as slick-talking, cool residents of cutting-edge culture. In contrast, Mom and Dad are clueless, bumbling old people. Fathers especially are routinely personified as dolts, inept and ineffective. The natural order of healthy family life is turned inside out on TV.

Kids naturally think they know more than grown-ups. They don't need a bunch of TV grown-ups telling them they're right.

Advertising Rules

Advertising isn't always content to sell just the benefit of its product or even the self-esteem that supposedly comes with it. It often

---

[24] Michael Medved, *Hollywood vs. America: Popular Culture and the War on Traditional Values* (New York: HarperCollins, 1992).

sells a philosophy of life, and not a good one. That's fine with the ad people, as long as it works.

Ad-based cultural propaganda hit the scene a few decades ago. The message: Rules, boundaries, standards, authority—bad. Ignoring, defying, challenging them—good. The admirably rebellious, autonomous self knows to resist constraints. Constraints belong in the moral dustbin of the past.

The slogans are tirelessly repetitive. Still, the ad designers get big bucks for concocting them. "Life without limits." "Imagine a world without limits." "No limits." "To know no boundaries." "Sometimes you gotta break the rules." "No rules, just right." "We broke the rules." "This baby don't play by the rules."

The list is deep, but the counsel is shallow: Pay no attention to those who would inhibit your impulses. And use our stuff: It will help you do that.

Why is the ad industry so eager to tie their wares to such an "in your face" attitude? Thomas Frank, author of *The Conquest of Cool*, says that the sixties counterculture is now "a more or less permanent part of the American scene.... Rebellion is both the high- and mass-cultural motif of the age: Order is its great bogeyman."[25]

All this is but another sign of the ad pros' talent for reading the human psyche. Whether they're aware of it or not, or whether they'll admit it or not, they are playing to what the Christian faith calls "fallen human nature." They are pushing consumers toward their natural inclination, which is to challenge rules and limits. Their allure is to the self-ruling individual. And along the way, of course, they make money. But at whose expense? As usual, those who are less discriminating. Read: kids.

---

[25] Thomas Frank, *The Conquest of Cool: Business Culture, Counterculture, and the Rise of Hip Consumerism* (Chicago: University of Chicago Press, 1998), 228.

TV or Not TV

If "Break the rules" slogans earn big bucks for the agencies that coin them, maybe I could start writing slogans: Rule the rules; "No" is for wimps; Boundaries—made for rivers, not people. On second thought, my conscience would bother me. It has rules and limits.

Less TV means less ads. A good rule to embrace.

Room with a View

One survey found that 71 percent of kids ages eight to eighteen had a TV in their bedrooms. They surveyed mostly older kids, right? Not according to another survey, which said that close to the same percentage of third graders had a TV for a roommate.[26] A Dartmouth College survey of 6,500 boys and girls, ages ten to fourteen, found that 59 percent had room TVs. All the surveys concur: It's well more than half.

Other studies confirm the ill effects of TVs in kids' bedrooms: less reading, lower grades, poorer sleep, and weight gain. The picture is crystal clear, but not pretty.

If your child has a TV-less bedroom, you're in the minority. If it lacks both TV and computer, you're in a tiny minority. You're a parenting oddball. That doesn't mean you're wrong.

"His grandparents bought him a TV for his room." To paraphrase a comedian: "These are not the same people who raised us. These are older people now trying to get into heaven." While a grandparent may bemoan the slipping discipline of the younger generation, she may feel obliged to keep her own grandkids from feeling too unlike their peers. Consequently, she may strive to

[26] Jessica Kelmon, "Is There a TV in Your Child's Room?" Great-Schools.org, June 18, 2018, https://www.greatschools.org/gk/articles/effects-of-tv-in-children-bedroom/.

soften any social stunting brought about by her own children's parenting, which is obviously not moving with the latest trends. One grandparent asked, "If they don't watch TV, how will they know what's popular with their peers?" Their peers will tell them.

A mother told me that her mother bought a TV for her son's bedroom, along with the warning, "I bought it for him, and if you don't let him have it, you'll deal with me." Mom abhorred the idea of a TV in her son's room, but she felt cornered. To sustain a fragile peace, she yielded. She asked if I thought she had the right to reject something that anyone — in this case, her mother — had given her son.

I asked, "If a classmate gave him a bag of marijuana, would you confiscate it?"

"Of course."

"Why?"

"Because it's harmful to him."

"You've just answered your own question. You not only have the right but the duty to protect your son from bad influences (the TV, not Grandma), no matter what they are."

"But marijuana is illegal. A television isn't," she said.

"True, but both can do harm, just in different ways."

Call it the "relative rule." It states that all gifts from relatives, no matter how well-intentioned, are subject to your scrutiny and, if need be, your veto. The closer the family members, the more they might question or resist your decision. Nonetheless, even the closest family members don't automatically have the authority to override your judgment.

PG — When?

The producers of screen content finally showed a little responsibility toward families.

TV or Not TV

Filling the culture with entertainment from the wholesome to the wretched, they now offer a means, however fuzzy, to anticipate which might be which. Thus, the familiar rating systems for television programs. (That it wasn't needed not so long ago speaks volumes.)

Many parents give these ratings credibility. They use them to gauge what is safe for their children and what isn't, what upholds their values and what undercuts them — at least until they see the content associated with the ratings.

Not a few moms and dads have told me how they sat shocked at, walked out of, turned off, or threw away what they were led to believe was "age appropriate."

Age appropriate? Says who? Parents like them, or residents of the entertainment world? Are you confident that the raters think and believe as you do? That they would guard a child's eyes as you would? Answer: the Lichter-Rothman survey in chapter 1 of this book.

Watching movie trailers rated PG-13, I've often thought, "I wouldn't want my thirteen-year-old mugged by these words and images." They were rough enough for someone my age. Who considers this stuff all right for a thirteen-year-old?

Many years ago, I attended one of those popular dinosaurs-run-amok movies. It was rated PG-13, along with the warning that some scenes may be too intense for young children. As I stood in the packed lobby, I was surrounded by parents with children well under ten.

The ratings were telling the truth. During one particularly gory scene, my wife buried her face in my shoulder to hide her eyes. Seated in front of us was a young boy, looking no more than seven or eight. His reaction contrasted dramatically with my wife's: "Whoa! How cool!", as he practically jumped out of his seat.

It provided sad evidence of how a young child can be not only numbed but titillated by gore. It also showed that even loose Hollywood standards cease to deter some parents.

Should you be skeptical about the reliability of ratings, know that others in your social circle might not be. They may have few reservations about showing at their place what you wouldn't at yours. Playdates, birthday parties, sleepovers—all can be places for your child to absorb visual junk that would never be allowed to enter your front door.

No matter how well you think you know the host, always verify the entertainment. You won't have to learn through hard experience that you were mistaken about someone whose values you thought were like yours. And your child won't have to see something objectionable for you to learn that.

PG-13 says: "Some material may not be suitable for children." Not "isn't," but "may not." As in, "We won't definitely advise you against this for your kids." Good marketing—and ratings are marketing—leaves some wiggle room to attract a wider audience.

No way can you shut out everything that streams and screams your child's way. Not as the culture is now. Your aim is much more doable: It is to filter and limit what seeks your child's eyes. In so doing, you, not Hollywood, will be the executive director of her character.

TV Guides

Most poisons are dose dependent. The body may tolerate a small amount with few long-term ill effects. A little more will make you sick. Even more can be life-threatening. Toxic television is dose dependent. The more a child ingests, the more likely it is to cause harm—moral and psychological.

Little kids can see something scary or repulsive on TV and be emotionally shaken by it. They can't easily separate screen fantasy from reality. What may follow are insecurities, fears, or nightmares. Fortunately, time typically fades the image, as long as parents don't allow similar images to keep assaulting their children.

TV or Not TV

Growing up, I thought three channels was a TV buffet. Growing up, my children saw cable and satellite television hit the airwaves with dozens, then hundreds, of options — I couldn't keep count. It was more like an invitation to gluttony. Fortunately, the services also offered "password access" to those channels we wished to ban, which were most. It continues to be the best option.

Parents watching a recorded program with their children often are quick to fast-forward through scenes that are vile, bloody, or sexually graphic. The kids aren't fooled. They know some deplorable stuff is in there — and now they're curious. Will more such scenes be coming? Does watching the whole movie send a mixed moral message?

In my book *Back to the Family*, I quote a mother who promised her adolescent children: "Your dad and I have agreed not to watch anything we wouldn't allow you to watch." She wanted to make a strong statement: We will watch only what we allow you to watch.

There are parents who — to the amazement of all around them — disconnect or pitch the TV. They realize it has encroached way too much on family life. Or, that it is way too hard to supervise. Very few have reversed the move. Over time, they missed the set less and regained more of family life.

A total TV fast appeals to few families, though. In most, a TV diet is more palatable:

- No television on school days.
- No television after 8:00 p.m. or some other chosen hour.
- TV time must be purchased. Each half hour might cost twenty-five cents. Educational programs cost less — not because they're worth less, but because they're worth more.
- Chores earn television. For example, a half hour of chores earns a half hour of parent-approved television. Be ready, Oscar may try to negotiate for a more

profitable ratio—say, one minute of chores for every hour of TV. Inflation, you know.

Re-View

Television will teach your children attitudes, morals, and behaviors absolutely opposed to yours. And it won't always be up-front about it. Much will enter your home under the guise of harmless entertainment. In its youth, TV talked and showed ideals allied with those of most parents. It now hard-sells its view of how the world should be.

Violence, unrestrained sex, twisted reality—sounds like a promo for a critically acclaimed new series, doesn't it? These are the staples of envelope-pushing TV. If it smells, it sells.

Kids believe their parents would see life more sharply with youthful eyes. Television tells them, "You're right. To get a savvy, slick-talking perspective, turn to the kids."

Is TV in a bedroom smart? Is it even okay? No. In print, my answer looks calm. Out loud, it would be NOOO!! It's tough enough to control a television sitting in plain sight. It's even tougher when it's hiding in a child's sanctuary.

Others can decide when and how much to live in television's world. They have that right. They don't have the right to question you for living in your world, one without much TV.

9

Over Stuffed

The numbers are big and not pretty: The national debt, the years
since my hometown team won a World Series, the amount of debris
on a teen's bedroom floor, the sum of advertisements bombarding
a child.

Only the last two directly impact your family—unless you also
root for my forlorn baseball team. The ruined-room clutter will
be picked up shortly. First, let's dig our kids out from under the
avalanche of ads burying them.

One estimate is that children see and hear more than twenty
thousand ads every year. Another doubles that to forty thousand
—on television alone, pushed along by sixteen minutes of ads per
primetime hour. Whatever the number, one thing is certain: It's
large.

Anything that saturates our senses becomes a casualty of its own
repetition. Some proportion of all this advertising gets muted, if not
blocked, by our sensory defenses (see chapter 1). Not everything
that seeks to persuade us does so. That's the good news.

The bad news: Through overwhelming our environment, advertising penetrates. While it pinches your pocketbook, it messes
with your child's character.

Raising Upright Kids in an Upside-Down World

A Malleable Audience

Advertising once primarily targeted adults, kids having neither the interest nor the money to spend. That's not the scene anymore. Kids are their own marketing segment. The older kids now have cash, and the ad people are sprinting after it.

Further, the young are a pliable audience. They can't so readily discriminate the legitimate from the oversold. The American Academy of Pediatrics bluntly asserts: Kids under eight are "cognitively and psychologically defenseless against advertising." Put simply, "Seeing is believing."

When I was a boy (funny how more of my sentences are starting this way), the cool cartoons were Bugs Bunny, Popeye, Road Runner, Tom and Jerry, Rocky and Bullwinkle. Though they pitched kid-pleasing products, the cartoons themselves sought to entertain, not to sell.

Kid programs today often are thinly cloaked infomercials, peddling games and action heroes that walk, talk, and can make your bed. The intent is to create a real-life craving for the on-screen fantasy — and every item the marketers can imagine with the characters' images splashed on them. What nine-year-old, gripped by hyperactive animation, will tell his mother, "See what they're doing? I see it. They want me to nag you for this stuff. How dumb do they think I am?" It's proven: The more watched, the more wanted.

Every Christmas shopping season — starting on schedule, the morning after Halloween — ads extol the hottest and latest, provoking a predictable stampede to snag the first of a "limited supply." (How come limited supplies never run out?) It would be hard to find a more potent example of ad muscle strong-arming parents.

Fed up, one father resolved never to buy anything for his kids at its group-think peak, knowing that within a few months, passion for the product would cool. Before too long, it would be shelved behind the next must-have novelty.

Don't misread me. This isn't grinchy advice to reject anything that's new and nifty. Toys surge and fade, faster every year. And some of them are ingenious, destined to be classics. I still have my electric football game from Christmas of my fifth-grade year. Rather, be attuned to all the commercial cajolery aimed at your kids, seeking to breed greed. Reducing their screen time will automatically reduce their cravings. As my wife used to say, "They won't know what they're supposed to ask for."

Master Psychologists

The old, reliable ad formula was: "Here is our product; here is what it does; here is why it's superior." It was an unvarnished pitch about the positives of purchase.

Most ad pros are not psychologists. Still, they are masters at reading the human psyche. They've learned that they can boost product appeal by merging it with self-esteem. "Get our brand: People will like you; you will stand out; you will be happier." Personal growth is but a buy away. Similar claims once belonged only to traveling patent medicine shows — snake oils and the like.

G. K. Chesterton, an author and clear-eyed social observer, long ago declared that the American people were too savvy to be tricked by such transparent mental manipulation. It may have been one of the few times Chesterton missed the mark.

For decades, psychologists have spouted the "virtue" of positive self-esteem, theorizing that it's linked to a child's full well-being. It's no surprise, then, that advertising takes advantage of this supposed connection. It targets a child's natural impulse to feel good about himself and to follow ever-shifting peer preferences. The message has evolved from "Here's something better" into "Here's something better for your self-image." It's the "new and improved" ad formula.

Raising Upright Kids in an Upside-Down World

When a child's self-image is tied to having more and better things, it will be fragile. It will be hostage to (what he is told is) the latest acquisition needed for his happiness and self-worth.

True self-worth can't be bought. It derives from hearing and believing that one is an infinitely valuable child of God. God is the master psychologist, not those who define a child by what he can possess next.

Grated by Ingratitude

"What quality would you most want your child to possess?" Parents routinely answer, "Gratitude." That is, a deep-felt appreciation for all one has and receives every day. Gratitude, unfortunately, is not a quality routinely acquired in a society that has so much of everything and continues to stretch for more.

My parents were raised during the Great Depression and World War II. They grew up living with lack, though they didn't think so then. As adulthood arrived, they moved materially ahead of their parents. Still, they never forgot what they once didn't have. The memories of their past nurtured their gratitude for their present.

Growing up, I never knew the scarcity my parents knew as children. I benefited from their rising standard of living. Likewise, my children benefit from my standard of living. They have more perks and possessions than I did as a child, and well more than their grandparents did.

It is indisputable: We have progressed into the wealthiest society in world history—materially, anyway. We have food in abundance and variety far beyond that of past emperors and kings; we have dwellings larger and finer than the vast majority of earth's people and wardrobes so jammed that whole racks can be mothballed merely for being declared by fashion gurus as "out of date"; we have air conditioning and heating that keeps temperature pleasant in house, car, job, anyplace; we have a multitude of cars, appliances, TVs, phones, tools, devices — you name it. Our pets are better kept and fed than many of the world's children.

All of this can be summed up with one word: luxury. Though we, and, more so, our kids, wouldn't call it that. We're accustomed to it. It's what's expected. It's life as it has come to be.

The most ordinary childhood activities are now paired with on-the-spot booty. Marlin gets his hair cut and gets to reel in a rubber fish from the salon's treat dispenser. Gideon can recite his Bible verse, so he can pick from the class treat bag. Wendy eats at a restaurant and along with her food comes a coloring book, balloons, cookies, stickers, and a matching 401(k). Trophies are granted just for showing up and playing the game — no keeping score, though. With a little planning and hoarding, a kid could schedule his own monthly yard sale.

My daughter Hannah liked to read. Early into first grade, she had already amassed forty-nine novelty erasers, one "earned" for each book she finished. As eraser mountain grew, her mother and I decided to erode it. Hannah was to pick her two favorites and return the rest. Our rationale: One, reading is its own reward. Two, forty-nine is forty-seven too many. We assumed Hannah brought the erasers back, as we never did see them again. Her teacher probably thought we were some sort of book burners. Nah, just eraser returners.

One small step toward teaching gratitude is gently to refuse some of the stuff that deluge your child. Brace yourself, though: You won't hear cheers, from your kids or from the goodie-giving grown-ups.

No Applause for You

Those of you with younger children, do an experiment. At a fast-food restaurant, order a "kids' meal" and tell the server, "No toy, please." After the "Huh? What did you just say?" gaze, you'll get a sympathetic, "With all the kids' meals, the toy comes free. You don't pay for it." Of course you do. And notice the unspoken, "How could you actually refuse something that's free?"

So, you explain, "Thank you, but we don't really need another toy." And the server is thinking, "'We'? The toy isn't for you." You could explain further, "I think eating out and ordering from a list of food is a big treat " Probably better to keep that to yourself. The server already wonders about your license to raise kids.

(Besides, what happens to this trinket at home? You step barefoot on it for two weeks. You sneak it into the trash at 2 a.m. and cover it with coffee grounds, only to hear the next morning, "Hey! How did that get in there? I got only twenty-four of those. That was my favoritest one, too!")

With your continued refusal, the server's sympathy becomes stunned silence, as he turns a commiserating face toward your empty-handed child, as though he's a waif from *Oliver Twist*.

Ask a departing question: "Have you ever had anybody refuse the toy?" "Not really," along with, "And I've worked here for a while." Of the countless parents who have ordered kids' meals, you're the first weirdo to pass up the toy.

A grandparent called me about his ten-year-old granddaughter. Her school held a year-end track "Olympics," and at day's end, all the participating children received a trophy. She declined hers, telling her teacher, "I don't need that. I didn't win any races. I'm just not a real fast runner." A gratuitous self-put-down? Not according to Grandpa, who said his granddaughter acknowledged her foot speed, or lack thereof, and really didn't want a trophy because she didn't earn one.

I was impressed by this ten-year-old's insight. Her teacher must not have been, as she later asked Grandpa about the girl's "self-image issues." Apparently, even kids confuse grown-ups if they don't run with the "stuff for all" competition. I suggested that Grandpa give his granddaughter a trophy for her maturity. Or at least a sticker.

Grand Largesse

It's a stereotype, but it has truth: Grandparents like to spoil their grandchildren. "Cookie, I told you before, you always have to finish your ice cream before I give you another piece of cake." They have the means and motive to give—lots.

When I asked my father for a twenty-five-cent raise in allowance, I first had to complete a six-page financial disclosure form, submit a budget, and listen to a lecture on fiscal discipline. But when I had kids of my own and Dad walked into our house, he'd announce, "Any children living here need Grandpa dollars?" His relaxed monetary policy had little to do with inflation.

Grandparents typically are moved by love: "Gifts show I care; I want them to have more than I did; I like to see them excited; I'm able now to give more." Good intent regularly leads to going overboard.

Grandparents don't limit their largesse to special occasions such as birthdays, Christmas, Groundhog Day. Any time is prime time for grandma or grandpa gifts.

GRANDMA: Look at this cute little stuffed zebra I picked up for Kitty at a yard sale.

PARENT: Mom, it's nice, but her bed is already buried in the stuffed animals you've bought for her.

GRANDMA: I know, but she doesn't have a zebra. I saw an open spot for it down by the foot of her bed.

PARENT: Mom, she has seven horsey animals.

GRANDMA: Did you see how big they are? This one is tiny and a lot easier to carry around. She can keep it in the car.

PARENT: Have you looked in our car? We have five stuffed animals in there.

GRANDMA: Yes, but I noticed they're all in the back seat. There aren't any in the front seat.

Okay, I'm exaggerating. Sort of. There are only three in the back seat.

Losing Weight

You want to be respectful and thankful, particularly toward family and friends. Yet you're uneasy with the excess. How do you strike a balance?

Explain yourself. "We're really trying to cut back on what the kids are getting from everywhere. It's too much. We want them to be more appreciative. We know how much you like getting them things, but we want them to love you for you and not for what you can buy." In other words, their presence is more valuable than their presents.

Thin the herd. For some years, I advised parents, "Purge half the glut." I've come to realize that's not always good advice. My chosen fraction is now closer to two-thirds. Kids with too much don't even notice a 50 percent shrinkage. Much of their surplus is worn out, broken, missing parts, or buried in the back of a closet.

If Bunny has stockpiled sixteen stuffed animals—not counting those in the car—and you free half of them, she still has eight left. How many does she need to feel fulfilled?

To control our home's menagerie, we set a policy: Two animals per bed—the stuffed kind, that is. When a third comes in, choose your favorite. All extras are given away. Over time, our policy loosened a bit. The younger kids quietly gathered three or four. The older kids must have kept a log of which animals they surrendered and when, as they were quick to confront us with documentation of our parenting slippage.

Over Stuffed

Possessions come fast and stay long. They grow like mold. Every so often, they have to be scrubbed out. That guards against hoarding. It also makes your house seem bigger.

Make thinning a joint exercise. Together, you and the kids decide what gets kept, pitched, or donated. If there's no consensus, yours is the tie-breaking vote. At a hospital, the volunteer staff will marvel at your kids' kindness. Hopefully, they won't give them a "Super Kid" plaque or a trophy that says, "I'm the best." Don't confess that you coerced some of their altruism.

Apply the relative rule, introduced last chapter: You have the final say in what is acceptable from anyone—relative or not—based on your values, your child's innocence, or merely the amount of stuff already accumulated. In short, for any reason you believe best.

Will you hear, "You know, I really admire you. Raising grateful kids is tough these days, and it's great to see a parent taking a stand against excess. Your kids will buy into your thinking—if not now, someday"? Should someone regale you with anything even close to this, thank her profusely, and buy her a little gift while you're at it.

Be gracious and grateful. It shows respect. Even more so, it helps keep relationship peace. Acceptance doesn't imply a promise to keep. Should the giver find out you didn't keep, she could feel slighted and think you're being ungrateful. You're not. Your intent is to teach your kids gimme control. That supersedes any obligation to keep something because it was given, even with the best of intentions. Will your kids tattle on you? Mine did.

Think of the gift's life expectancy. In a short while, will it be ignored, discarded, regifted, or sold for a dollar at a yard sale? If so, you're just accelerating its aging process.

Do you have the right to take ownership of a gift meant for your child? Why wouldn't you? You would have no qualms refusing something that is illegal or immoral. What if it doesn't align with your goals as a parent? What if it doesn't benefit your child's character?

In fact, you control your kids' wants all the time. You stop Chip from grabbing a fourth cookie. You collect the remote from Nielson after he's watched two hours of TV. You give Forbes a ten-dollar-a-week allowance, not twenty-five, as he thinks is fair. Denying bad things is good parenting. So is denying good things in bad quantity.

Rebalance Christmas. Noelle gleefully pounces upon her first present on Christmas Eve. She's excited to savor it, but a stack beckons. After a few gifts, she's in a shark-like feeding frenzy, pausing only long enough to grab the next one on the pile.

Slow the tempo. Decelerate the rush to "What's next?" Make time for Noelle to show appreciation. A direct thank-you to each giver after each gift, walking over, a hug—all show gratitude better than a generic "thanks" to all after the wrap-up.

If you believe the gift deluge is too heavy, set aside some for after-Christmas opening. Or, to really test Noelle's beneficence, you and she could bring the gifts to a nearby hospital, where there are young patients whose only Christmas visitors are the staff.

The Landfill

"I won't step into his room without hazmat gear." "Two of her sisters accidentally stumbled into her bedroom two days ago. We haven't found them yet." "I call his room 'Star Trek'—to venture in is to boldly go where no mom has gone before."

The experts say: It's his room. It's a personal space. Just close the door. Pick your battles.

Yes, it is his room—sort of. It's in your house. And you may want to avoid citations for multiple health-department violations. Should you opt to "just close the door," make it a steel one with a four-inch external dead bolt. Animals can gnaw through wood.

Other parents say: "All kids' rooms look that bad. It's their age." "I found it just wasn't worth the fight." "Compared with my daughter's room, your daughter's room looks like the White House greeting room."

Whether experts or other parents, the underlying thinking is the same: It's common; therefore, it's normal. And if it's normal, it's acceptable. Because 73 or 82 or 94 of 100 teens' bedrooms fall below city health codes in no way means your Dusty's has to be one of them. Tolerable room conditions for other parents may not be so for you.

Why are kids and tidy bedrooms such a mismatch? Some reasons are obvious: apathy, laziness, comfort with chaos, the assumption that somebody else (read: parent) will clean it, too much else to do. Uh huh.

One reason is not so obvious: Too much of most everything. If Barbie had one doll instead of eight, would she care for it better? If Jordan had one good pair of basketball shoes, not five, would he guard it more closely? If Taylor's wardrobe weren't ever-expanding, would she be more or less inclined to hang up her clothes? The correlation between more stuff and less gratitude, particularly when the stuff comes freely and easily, is clear. The correlation between more stuff and less responsibility is a little less direct, but it's present and it's potent.

Reclaiming the Landfill

Reducing the amount of stuff finding refuge in Dusty's refuse should help slowly restore some order. What about in the meantime? You could threaten to rent a backhoe to haul out the rubble. Or you could multiply air fresheners throughout the house to neutralize the sock smell wafting into the kitchen. Here are a few more sanitizing strategies.

1. Declutter Dusty's room yourself, but charge for your time. You're union wage, aren't you? What about overtime? Do you have a recycling fee?

2. Armed with a heavy-duty trash bag, enter Sandy's sanctuary. Warn her that you will be sorting through the mess, and you can't be sure what is valuable and what isn't. Anything could end up in your bag.

3. Anytime Clay asks for some freedom, ask back, "How does your room look?" The privilege is linked to the state of the room. A clean room doesn't guarantee a yes, as Clay might assume. A dirty room does guarantee a no.

4. Schedule inspection times; for example, Wednesday at 6:00 p.m. and Saturday at 10:00 a.m. The room meets your standards, or Heloise stays in there until it does.

5. Fine Penny for each day her room is not fine. Use the payments to help offset any depreciation on your house.

There is a bonus to an overloaded, undermaintained room: If you run out of storage space in the garage, you can always park the lawn tractor in there. Forest will never notice it.

Re-Collect

Ours is a wealthy, luxurious society. By the world's standards, present and past, our lifestyle is lavish. The dominant narrative is: Here is more. More is good. Lots more is best.

The ad pros know that children, and thus their parents, are a ready audience. They create craving by creating a steady supply of new "needs."

Family and friends, however well-meaning, can over-give. And kids receive all sorts of trinkets, goodies, and "rewards" just for living everyday life.

All of this counters the teaching of gratitude. Gratefulness grows slowly, if at all, when too much comes too freely, too fast.

Keep your hand on the spigot. Turn it down as much as you believe is best. Just because so much is easily acquired in no way means that you must let your child acquire it. Restoring material sobriety will lead many, young and old, to misunderstand you, to label you a descendant of Scrooge.

But this may just be the price of giving your child the ultimate gift — gratitude.

10

Circles of Influence

An IQ of 140 is not normal. Less than 1 percent of the population would score this high. Perfect pitch — the ability to identify musical tones without any training — is even rarer. About one in ten thousand people are born with it. Few, of course, would regard a high IQ or perfect pitch as a liability. Rather, both are deemed assets.

A theme of this book is: The better you parent, the less "normal" you are. You do not follow prevailing standards. This is not to say those who do are necessary substandard parents. An IQ of 115 is high; it's just not as high as 140. Most skilled musicians lack perfect pitch. They're still talented.

If you don't parent like most, it follows: Most don't parent like you. What cultural pulls you resist, they might not. Their childrearing IQ, if you will, may be closer to the average of 100. Your aim is a childrearing IQ much higher than average. Say, 140?

Kids of Influence

"Bad influence": It's how a parent might describe someone who encourages his child toward conduct that is sneaky, defiant, or immoral. Most parents wouldn't be slow to curtail or to end the influence. No matter their child's opposition, they would act decisively. The smart move is obvious.

The smart move might not be quite so obvious when a peer is less a "bad" influence and more a "worldly" one. That is, he has been raised closer to cultural norms than has your child. He has had more liberties—social, technological, material—at an earlier age than yours. And he might not be older than your child. He could be younger.

Whether another child's influence is bad, worldly, or some mix of both, an involved parent faces the question: How much contact, if any, do I permit?

Picky Parents

"You can't pick my friends," declare teens. "You can't pick their friends," declare experts. One wonders if they've raised any teens.

"You can't pick my friends" is, pardon my lack of diplomatic counselor speak, utter nonsense. It's a bullying tactic to make you second-guess yourself and to forgo your God-given duty to monitor your youngster's whereabouts and who-abouts. It insists, "My social life is my business, not yours!" Excuse me?

Your son, Noble, wants to cavort with Conan, who just broke the school record for detentions and is pleading "no contest" to multiple vandalism charges. How strongly would you object to Noble's picking Conan as a friend? Would you, with haste, remove him from Noble's buddy list?

Granted, you can't interview and vet every one of Noble's associates. No doubt, there are a few he chooses that you wouldn't, though your misgivings aren't solid enough to act—yet. Still, you have the right and the responsibility, when you judge wise, to narrow his options. Put another way, you can't pick each friend, but you can pick the pack from whom he can pick.

In fact, you direct your child's choices all the time. Fruit for breakfast, not donuts; nice pants to church, not ripped shorts; bed at 10 p.m., not midnight; half of money to savings, not to online poker. In all sorts of things, you are a far better picker than Flip.

Aren't kids social beings? Yes. Do they gather in groups? Yes. Isn't the push and pull of peer relations part of maturing? Yes. Won't kids sort out on their own who's a good companion and who isn't? No, not always.

Because Amity desires to socialize, it doesn't follow that socializing of any kind is always desirable. It matters utmost with whom she socializes.

Draw a parallel to literacy. Some argue that because reading is good for a child, what he reads is secondary, as long as he is reading something. No: Reading bad things can have bad effects. Worldly friends can have the same.

Who's Judging?

"You're judging my friends." The "J" word, reflexively flung at anyone who makes any assessment about right or wrong, good or bad, smart or dumb.

The word "judgmental" has been badly twisted out of shape. It has come to mean making any assessment other than unquestioning acceptance. To say anything that sounds negative or even less than fully affirming about anyone or anything is asking to be tagged with the "J" word.

Is judging another child's conduct judging her as a person? Is it slandering her or her family? Is it claiming that you and yours are superior people who shouldn't sully yourselves with the likes of her?

The answer to each of these is a resounding no — though a teen may answer with a resounding yes. Not because he fully believes what he's saying, but because he's flinging any argument at hand to change your mind. He's pushing hard to be allowed to "hang with" someone you judge—there's that word again—not good to "hang with."

"Don't judge my friends" is akin to "You can't pick my friends." Both are unthinking mantras barely rooted in reason or reality. "You're judging" is a kid's go-to accusation should a parent express any cautions or concerns about a peer.

Being a parent makes you responsible for people other than yourself. You are called to make countless judgments for your children's well-being. If that is being judgmental, then being judgmental is good—full stop.

Clandestine Companions

To paraphrase an old movie line: A parent's got to know his limitations. One limitation every parent, even the most vigilant, understands: You are neither all seeing nor all knowing. A parent learns this about himself acutely during his teen's years. A child learns this about his parents during his preschool years.

Nothing yet invented can expand a youngster's circle of "friends" further and faster than a phone. Is the size of the circle, though, the measure of social health? Or is it who populates the circle? Further, a phone circle is easy to close, with "no admittance" to a parent.

Technology safeguards can keep Robyn from flying freely all over the Internet or social media. Her calls and texts, however, are much harder to track. "Syncing" her phone to yours is really the only sure way to get inside her circle to know who comes and goes. This is not stunting her social growth. It's extending your awareness.

A circle of in-school companions, if not altogether closed to you, may be mostly so. Stanford spends around thirty-five hours a week at school, or about 30 percent of his weekday waking hours. Who exactly travels within his circle is hard to know, unless his younger sister travels the same halls and is eager to give you reports. Can you shadow Ford to see whom he walks with, talks with, eats with? His sister could, but they've spotted her tailing them already.

You don't have to be a distant, passive parent, however. Ford may roam the school with Harley, but that doesn't mean you have to allow him to roam with Harley elsewhere. His in-school movements may be beyond your reach. His out-of-school movements are not.

Risky traveling companions sometimes drive off on their own. Harley may decide your school-zone speed limits are way too slow for him. It's time to seek other traveling companions whose parents aren't part-time police.

Again, you are not picking each and every one of Ford's friends. You are picking what freedoms he can pursue with which friends.

Neighbors and Friends

Social psychologists cite "proximity" as a major producer of friendships. Meaning, friendships are more likely to evolve in shared environments — school, work, church, teams.

For kids, the neighborhood is a shared environment. It's a source of playmates, though the numbers filling it have dropped markedly in the past couple of generations. The once-familiar scene of kids bunching in yards or bikes bunching in driveways has been replaced by bunches of virtual games. Still, kids have energy to burn, and parents need respites, so outside activities do happen — more so when a parent limits inside activities.

My son Andrew was about eight years old when three brothers from a nearby house saw him in our yard and ventured over. After greeting and talking with the boys, I sensed I had better keep an eye on the goings-on. The first few innings of their impromptu ball game confirmed my initial impressions: The brothers, even the youngest one, were more culturally "grown up" than Andrew.

What were my options? Umpire the game? Cancel the game? Be steady pitcher for every game? Allow only inside play with an adult less than ten feet away? Pay Andrew's six-year-old sister to oversee the boys?

All of these had drawbacks. I couldn't monitor everything. At best, my wife or I could make periodic checks. And Andrew's sister was expensive: She charged by the person. On one hand, I wanted the boys to feel welcome at our place. On the other, I wanted to protect Andrew's eight-year-old innocence. How to balance both?

A resolution: The boys were welcome, provided they played by our rules for language, behavior, and disputes, the last of which are rife in boys' pickup competitions. From all we could see and hear, they did, with only sporadic hiccups. Over the months, though, the boys slowly trickled away, with the games becoming fewer and farther apart. Apparently, they outgrew Andrew and his parents' "little boy" rules.

Did Andrew ask to go to their place? More than once. Was he allowed? Nope. Because the boys' parents were separated, they were living with their grandparents. They were pleasant people, but appeared overwhelmed by the demands of raising children the second time around, this time with an omnipresent computer, TV, and virtual games. Over there, Andrew would be under their rules, which were mostly shaped by the boys' rules.

Setting boundaries on younger neighbors can create disharmony with older neighbors — that is, their parents. Who wants strained relations with those living less than a hundred yards away? Sadly, depending on the width of the worldliness gap between their children and yours, you may have no good solution. You may have only a less bad one: Curtail or completely suspend contact between the families. Do you have a second residence in Maui?

Will the neighbors understand? Perhaps not. They don't think your Chastity is all that innocent either. She causes her share of the trouble. At least that's what their Lulu has told them. They may assume you think your family superior and theirs deficient. In acting positively for your child, other parents can interpret it as a negative judgment on them or their children. Be reassured, though: Relations can become more neighborly with time. (After Lulu leaves for college?)

Relative Differences

The dynamics quickly become more ticklish when involving a member of one's own family — cousins, in-laws, grandparents. An older sibling? To remove all potential for trouble, a parent may decide to shun the relative. More often than not, this creates more problems than it solves. It foments family friction, with people taking sides and distancing themselves from one another.

A less drastic option: Practice "enhanced situational awareness," as law enforcement terms it. This is a heightened alertness to one's surroundings — or, for a parent, her child's surroundings. What is Butkus doing right now? Who is with him? Where are they? Is that the sound of someone being kicked?

Situate yourself in a strategic place to look and listen and, if need be, move fast. We adults can get quickly immersed in our grown-up conversations, forgetting to check periodically on the kids.

One mother, when her instincts alerted her to brewing kid trouble, quietly removed her son from the scene, even if he wasn't actively involved. It wasn't to discipline him. Rather, it was a preemptive move. She stepped in before the problems gained momentum. She explained her actions to him later.

Older kids at family events like to slip off to adult-free zones to circle around whoever's device is the coolest and latest. Those zones are best considered off-limits. Better yet, invoke "Grandma's rule." All devices are surrendered at your door. Your niece, Star, may give an attitude that says, "No phone, no me." Would that solve your problem?

Your relative admires your Angelica, even as she questions your "too strict" ways. She considers her a good influence on her children, so she wants them all to spend time together.

Notice the contradiction? You are "too strict," but your child is a good influence. As one father pondered, "Am I too strict, or do I have a great kid? I don't think it can be both."

Your relative is anything but strict. Her child-rearing style is much more "hands off" than yours, and her kids reflect it. As an aside, when a parent is "hands off," others' hands will eventually do the molding and disciplining.

Up to now, you've been answering most of her overtures with dubious dodges, but your reluctance is becoming more noticeable. Instead of assorted excuses, try: "Thank you, but we are doing everything we can to get more family time. We don't have nearly as much as we'd like." Few people can argue that families these days aren't pulled in twelve directions at once.

If you homeschool, prepare to hear, "But you're with them all day. Don't you want a break?" Say, "I do, but I'm real picky about who I leave them with." Okay, don't say that, unless you'd rather not hear from your relative for a long while. Instead, "That sounds good. Let's all get together. When is a good time?" You'll find out if she likes your company as well as Angelica's. If so, you'll also guarantee the presence of at least one "hands on" adult.

A Grand View

"My parents let our kids watch TV shows at their house that they know I don't approve of." Whether they realize it or not, your parents are broadcasting to your kids, "Your parents are too uptight. We'll loosen things up here." Not only are they subtracting from your authority at their place, but they're adding static at yours, as your kids tune in to your being not as TV-cool as Grandma and Grandpa. They're grown-ups too, you know, ones who've been around a lot longer than you. They should have the better view of what's good to watch and what's not.

Your parents don't have to agree with your TV guidance; they just have to agree that *you* are your kids' TV guide. How do you ensure they will? What if they and the kids form a sort of silent conspiracy, allies of the screen?

You have an ally: your kids' at-home behavior. Kids aren't good at keeping secrets long. What they watch will be re-aired in their actions, as they begin to imitate mannerisms and language native to television but foreign to your home. Emmy's conduct will give you a picture of what she may be visually imbibing at her grand-parents' house.

If little changes, despite your repeated pleas, your parents have channeled you into a corner. Now you have to watch not only your kids, but them, too. The only certain way to do both is to always accompany Emmy and Oscar to Grandma and Grandpa's. For now at least, their solo visits may have to be canceled, unless you're willing to exchange your TV ratings for theirs.

"Honor your father and mother" means giving them the love and respect that is their due. It doesn't mean abiding by their every opin-ion or directive. Nor does it mean raising your kids as they raised you.

When your parents raised you, the culture was more friendly—or at least less hostile—to their values. Thus, they may be in a bit of a generational time lag, not perceiving the moral minefield of the culture quite as clearly as you do. They see few problems with helping their grandkids fit in a little better with it. You turned out fine, after all.

A grandparent may personify unconditional love. That doesn't mean she can't misread the times.

Miseducated Siblings

Your budding adult has returned home from college. He is sound-ing, for the moment anyway, as if he is holding many of the culture's ideas in higher esteem than yours. And he's feeling duty-bound to share his dawning "enlightenment" with others, especially his younger siblings.

What and how Oxford thinks may be impervious to your best arguments. He feels a growing independence, along with a pre-rogative to think "independently." That is his choice. It is not his choice, though, to re-educate a younger brother or sister.

If Oxford won't stifle his preaching, he's talking you into act-ing: loss of his car, phone, computer, money, any or all of these. He might claim adult status, but that's a legal claim. You still have lots of financial claims.

He may accuse you of abridging his First Amendment right to free speech. So you are. His freedom to speak doesn't include the free-dom to push his "reformed" values on his "unenlightened" siblings.

Talk to your younger kids. What have they heard from big brother? What questions did it raise? What is most confusing them? What don't they understand about what you've always taught them? You have little to fear from the college "lessons" of an older sibling. Yours are life lessons, decades in formation; his have percolated for a few years at most.

After one of our sons moved out, he found freedom intoxicating. He embraced his license to "think for himself," which really meant not thinking like Mom and Dad. And during family gatherings he felt no compunction about collaring his siblings and sharing his views. We asked him to keep them to himself. He didn't, so he wasn't invited to the next family event. We didn't want to exclude him. We just wanted to set boundaries on his proselytizing. Any exclusion would be *his* doing. After a couple of missed get-togethers, he returned — as a brother, not a philosopher-authority.

Know Better

It's a standard television news scene: The cameras roam the neighborhood, fixing their eyes on the neighbors of the "quiet family man" who was just arrested for a string of burglaries. Each resident echoes the next: "He seemed like a real nice guy—always waved when he drove by our house. At our last barbecue, he sent over a dozen ears of corn. I guess you never really can know, huh?"

Not exactly true. You can know—better, anyway. But it takes more time and more interactions across more situations.

Someone might compliment me after a parenting presentation: "You must be a great dad." I'm tempted to answer, "I hope so, but you can't know that. I may have sounded good the past hour, but that doesn't mean I act the same at home." Instead, I say something like, "Thanks, but you'll have to get my wife and kids to vote on that. They live with me every day." If someone says, "I'll bet you're a good dad," I might just smile. At least she's betting. She knows she could be wrong.

Of all those who move through our lives, we come to know well a small minority. Most others, we know at best a few inches deep.

We may have conversed with them, cheered beside them at our kids' games, volunteered together at school or church. Most social meetings, even regular ones, don't permit much penetration into someone's personality or morals.

People gravitate toward like-minded others. And parents, being people (despite what their teens at times may think), are no exception. It's natural. There is both comfort and confirmation in being with others who think as we do. There is also, however, a creeping bias—that is, we may be inclined to think that they think more like we do than they do.

"They seem like very nice people." They could well be. Being nice, though, doesn't translate to looking at life as you do or parenting as you do. What they find acceptable for their kids to have, see, and do, you may not.

"I always talk with parents before I leave my child with them." That's a good start, but it doesn't ensure a good end. It's falsely reassuring to rely on a short interview to feel confident that another parent's oversight would equal one's own.

"I can't believe what my daughter watched over there." Or what she played. Or what she searched on the Internet. Or what social media she cruised. Or what other kids were there.

The hindsight question: Where was the parent?

Practice the three As: ask, assess, anticipate. Whatever the event, if you're not there, ask plenty of questions of the big people who will be: Will you be present the whole time? Do you know all the kids who are coming? What is your stance on phones? If there's a movie, what is it? Is the Internet secure? Do the kids plan to leave the house? Will you be going along? Ask any and all questions you need to get the most complete picture.

Some may hear your queries as an "interrogation" or a lack of trust. Others may be pleased to hear from a parent so involved. Whichever it is, you are neither being rude nor "cross-examining." No answers, no go. Weak answers, still no go. You need good information to make a good decision. And if what happens doesn't match the reassurance you received, you'll know better for next time.

Awake-Overs

A mother hosted a slumber party for her middle-school daughter and friends. All the girls arrived with phones, so Mom thought that it smart to collect them for the night. Several of the girls complied, though with a silent expression that said, "Is this really necessary?" A few balked, hiding their phones on their persons. Mom was just about to insist, until she caught her daughter's unspoken pleading glance, "Mom, please, don't make a scene." So she relented, not wanting, as she put it, "to embarrass my daughter." (How does having sound rules "make a scene"?)

A sleepover, being nocturnal by definition, is a venue for secretive conduct. Its other name—slumber party—is an oxymoron. The adults are the first to slumber, just when the kids are gearing up to party.

You can make a sleepover safer with a couple of preconditions. One, you know the host nearly as well as you know yourself—trusted relative, close friend, probation officer. Two, you are the host. You know your eyes will stay wide open. And you know your planned activities—board games; duck, duck, goose; Twister; Mother, May I? On second thought, the kids will probably doze off before you, if they even come.

College Re-Education Camp

More than forty years ago, I absorbed the "college experience." Did I fly into freedom? Face first. Did I come, go, sleep, and wake on my own cycle. Sure did. Did I chase fun? At a gallop. Did my home-taught standards undergo some mutations? Afraid so.

In the 1970s, my college experience was typical. These days, it wouldn't be. It would be judged too restrained, too tethered to my upbringing.

Not many would dispute that the college scene is degenerating rapidly. If surveys reflect reality, students are attending alongside several soul-ravaging classmates: binge drinking, drugs, hookup sex, profligate partying. Some kids pilot through the shoals and graduate afloat. Many—surveys say over half—pass their courses but within a few years flunk the faith and morals taught to them for nearly two decades.

Raising Upright Kids in an Upside-Down World

Not all that long ago, institutes of "higher learning" (a questionable description?) embraced the concept of *in loco parentis*—"in place of the parent," for those of you who shunned Latin in high school. They accepted the role discharged to them by parents. Most schools now practice *in absentia parentis*, allying with the students' wants over the parents'. Even as the parents pay most of the bills, their kids are chaperoned on a journey to self-defined moral regress.

"My daughter is set on attending school out of state." To use my sister's favorite retort when we bickered, "So?" Kids are set on all kinds of things—some good, some bad. Parents regularly have to veto the bad, or what they see as potentially bad. On paper, a preferred college may look good. In life, it may end up being dangerously bad.

Faith can be trusted solo on a three-week Bahamian cruise. Wiley needs to be watched when he ventures into the next room. One good predictor of how a child will behave during college is how she behaved during high school. It's not a perfect predictor, though, as the college experience can morally muddle even the best of kids.

Adding to the social and moral questions is the financial one. Who is the bank? You? That gives you the controlling vote in Jewel's school choices. If costs are shared, you still hold a governing vote. If Jewel is paying her own way—tuition, room and board, car, phone, curling iron—as a legal adult, she can attend wherever. If she ventures back for the summer, who's providing at-home support? If you, then, once more, you retain a voice, its volume matching your volume of support.

My oldest daughter was drawn to an all-female college in another state. Our stance: You live here, we pay most. You live there, you pay most. She enrolled there, with all expenses covered by ROTC, and she graduated as an army officer, which was the career she wanted.

Circles of Influence

Our other college-bound children commuted, learning a price-less life lesson along the way: No loans is good.

Speaking of money, statistics say that up to half of graduates aren't employed in their degree major, while they're loaded with loans stretching into social security. To buy a few years away from home, they reveled in quasi-independence, only to return home and to quasi-dependence. For many, college is no longer the career ladder it has been promised to be. And it certainly isn't their ladder to better character.

The "commute is better" rule has exceptions. Technical or specialized degrees might be available only at a distance, as might scholarships. Religious schools might support your values rather than counter them. All things considered, though, near-home higher education is superior at preserving a youngster's child-hood ideals—as well as your pocketbook. Have you considered home-colleging?

Re-Visit

Blunting anti-parent cultural messages is an ongoing challenge. So is blunting the influence of culture-shaped peers. Kids navigate toward, away from, and around every kind of peer contact—good, bad, wholesome, worldly. It's not possible to screen and monitor all of their associates. It is possible to monitor, and, if need be, restrict, what they pursue with these associates.

You're wise, and rightly cautious, to assume that most parents —even those you believe you know well—may not supervise your child as you would. Repeat, as needed, the three As: ask, assess, anticipate. Nothing can substitute for a willingness to be fully involved. And "involved" is not "intrusive."

College moves a young person forward in his education, but often backward in his morals. The "college experience" away from home, more often than not, ends up doing little good for child or parent. Most often, commuting is the preferred avenue to sustain a youngster in your—and his—values.

11

Standing Strong

The culture doesn't value your values. Its reigning rules for proper living are moving farther away ever faster. At times with barely cloaked tolerance, at times with overt hostility, it scorns your deepest-held convictions.

All this is becoming clearer to you. Consequently, you are getting better at anticipating and thwarting assaults on your child's innocence and character. You are standing stronger, knowing that perseverance should lead you one day to behold an exceptional young person, a one-in-a-hundred adult.

It should, but it may not always. Why not? Why does one child hear your voice above all others, while another listens to dissonant voices? From all you can tell, you are raising both if not identically then similarly. What makes one absorb your guidance while another questions it?

The Power of Temperament

Anyone raising more than one child faces a daily truth up close. From birth — conception, to be biologically correct — every child is uniquely internally wired. He possesses an inborn personality, a temperament that can affect how much he will clash or cooperate with others and with everyday life.

Joy enters the world with an agreeableness that says, "Why, hello, Mother. It's so nice to see you. Would you prefer me to sleep through the night on the first night home from the hospital or the second?" Spike crashes in screaming, "Ready or not, world, here I am," as he searches for a cigar.

Observe a litter of young pups. Before any training whatsoever, each puppy shows himself. One nips at any hand that comes too close. Another cowers near his mother at the mere shadow of one of those towering, two-legged creatures. A third eagerly scrambles away from mom to check out the culture—I mean, surroundings.

Children are not puppies. For starters, puppies are easier to toilet train, quicker to learn from discipline, and more grateful for treats. Like puppies, however, each child has predispositions—internal inclinations—that a parent has no hand in shaping but is still called to permeate with good character. Sometimes that makes for a breezy stroll through parenthood. Sometimes it makes for a tricky two-steps-forward, one-step-backward dance.

Way back when I attended college—Freud was a freshman when I was a senior—most theories emphasized the ways environment shaped personality. The unique physiology of each child entered in, but as a distant second. In the nature-versus-nurture competition, nurture scored the most points.

Decades of doing therapy have taught me that nature must be given its due. What people are like as adults often has temperamental seeds in childhood. An anxious grown-up may have been an anxious child. An eruptive spouse threw flash tantrums as a preschooler.

Decades of fatherhood have taught me firsthand all about temperamental diversity. Ten kids present a wild scattergram of personalities. One child, taciturn from the womb, when asked what he did on his first day of kindergarten, answered, in a moment of explosive self-revelation, "Stuff." Another detailed her first day in two to four hundred words per minute with gusts up to eight hundred. One would flip out if a sibling sneezed. Another was so sanguine that he didn't notice he had siblings for his first six years.

An easy-to-raise first child can fluff up your ego, as you think you're God's gift to parenthood. "I am not about to put all my knickknacks ten feet off the ground in cages armed with alarms just because I have a toddler. He knows that my no means no."

All goes smoothly until your second toddler comes along, spies your knickknacks, and cuts the alarm's wires with the scissors he pilfered from the locked drawer. He used the "good scissors," too.

Temperament certainly is not the full measure of who a child is or becomes. But it is a major contributor. And it demands recognition and respect.

But it is not all powerful. You are not at the mercy of your child's genetics—which are half yours, by the way. Nor are you relegated to being an observer, as the culture does its part while his brain chemistry does the rest. Were that so, years of conscientious parenting would add up to little more than a chance outcome, a child-rearing flip of the coin.

On the other hand, to believe yourself the sole cause of whatever your child seeks or accepts is every bit as false. You do not parent in a vacuum. Your guidance interacts with your child's inborn nature in intricate, often frustratingly mysterious ways.

After years of your best efforts, should your child veer from his upbringing, you cannot and should not reflexively take the blame, scouring the past for where and how you fell short. You will batter yourself with undeserved guilt and self-rebuke. You do have great power to mute the culture's call, but how much a child is attracted to or repulsed by it depends also on his one-of-a-kind makeup.

Psychological Correctness

Modern parenting has come under the charge of "experts." We are everywhere—swarming the Internet, social media, and talk shows, all while pouring out endless articles and books. (Yes, I appreciate the irony.) We've swamped parents with a chorus—some would call it a cacophony—of voices for correctly talking, listening, reasoning, praising, disciplining, breathing. We have been granted "guru" status. We push no end of theories, techniques, and formulas for proper parenting.

The net effect has been to disorient, even intimidate parents: "Yes, you can muddle along, and with some luck, little Harmony won't need intensive therapy in her thirties. But to maximize success, follow the latest professionally certified child-rearing advice."

My name for this phenomenon is "psychological correctness." That is, there is a psychologically correct way to manage and respond to every child-rearing question or circumstance. Say the right words, use a savvy "I-message," set up a win-win scenario, and Dusty will brush his teeth before their color changes, Newton will complete his math homework before midnight, and Telly will agreeably concede, "You're right, Mother, all a smartphone would do at my age is change who I am, and not for the better."

The headlines shout: "Learn the 'secrets' to happy fulfilled child-rearing!" How did all those past generations, ignorant of these secrets, raise decent human beings?

Psychological correctness will undermine your authority and confidence. First, if you can be correct, then you can be "incorrect." Run counter to cultural trends, and you will find yourself in a minority, often a tiny one. It's easy to feel wrong when the numbers are stacked against you.

Second, who is the most correct? Experts (a.k.a., specialists, professionals, authorities) have letters after their names. Some have enough letters to spell another name. Do you take a letter count to determine whom to follow?

Can you poll one hundred experts to get a consensus on "how to" best handle a situation? You'd hear lots of disagreement. My advice: Consider as much advice as you wish, knowing the final decision is yours, based upon your child, your family, and your value system. You have accumulated a reservoir of common sense and instincts. Similar reservoirs helped guide thousands of generations. They're not out of date.

Third, many, if not most, experts don't think like you. They think more like the culture and its norms — experts are big on norms. They introduce and promote all kinds of novel notions. A sampling: Self-esteem trumps humility; high standards provoke rebellion; spanking is always and everywhere toxic; homeschooling stunts social skills; big families shortchange children.

All these are newcomers to the child-rearing scene. Parents throughout history wouldn't have heard of them, or, if they did, wouldn't have given them any credence. Did so many people from so many times and places get it so wrong? And in our day, did we finally manage to correct it?

Psychological correctness is a quagmire. It will dissolve your resolve to raise a child who doesn't reflect the culture but whom, ironically, many in the culture will admire.

Spiritual Correctness

Few parents feel more distressed and besieged by society's course than those whose faith in God is at the core of their family life. They face great pressure to compromise their most cherished beliefs in light of the culture's code. Shunning psychological correctness, they nevertheless may be ensnared by something similar: spiritual correctness. It says: If a parent does the spiritually good and right things, a child raised in the Faith will remain in the Faith. Teach godly morals, attend church, pray often, receive the sacraments, socialize in like-minded circles, educate in a religious or home school, live the example, and a child will seek God more fervently with age.

Certainly a God-centered family life is vital to raising a young person who hears God's still, small voice above the culture's din. It does not, however, guarantee it.

A parent may know in her head that she has no guarantees, yet in her heart feel that somehow, some way she fell short. More family devotions? Better moral instruction? Closer communication? Praying in Latin? Or Aramaic, the language of Jesus? She can't shake the sense that had she been just a little more religiously diligent, all would have ended up well.

Suppose you could consult with the master psychologist—Jesus. He could stand beside you and whisper perfect instructions into your ears all day long. That would raise a faith-seeking young person, wouldn't it? To answer this, here is a series of yes-or-no questions I ask parent groups.

Is there a God? Yes, they answer aloud.

Is Christ God? Yes.

Was He sinless? Yes.

Could He perform miracles? Yes.

Did He perfectly understand human nature? Yes.

I pause, letting all their answers settle in, then ask, "Could He get most people to follow Him?"

Pensively, the group responds, "No."

If the God-man Himself couldn't get most people to follow Him, why do we think we can, and should be able to, do better? I don't know about you, but I can't perform miracles. I can't do a two-bit card trick.

The upside to spiritual correctness: It can move a family toward more faith-filled living. The downside: It can move a parent toward feelings of failure when the outcome is not as expected. Do we think that we can live and teach so convincingly that a young person will have no choice but to follow our lead? In short, do I think that if I'm a saint, I will *always* raise a saint?

Too Late?

"I'm finally seeing how much the culture is undercutting my parenting. It's taken a long time. Is it too late?"

The saying is: We grow too soon old and too late smart. We can't stop growing older, but we can get smarter sooner. Smarter parenting comes from experience. Experience comes from making mistakes. Wisdom comes from correcting mistakes.

Young parents don't yet feel the full reach of the culture. Little Chastity is still safely nestled in their protective cocoon. They may sense its creep but underestimate its pace.

You may have once been culturally nearsighted, but your vision has improved. It's moving toward 20/20 — ideally, toward 20/15. Though it is sharpening later than you'd like, it is improving. Late is far better than never.

"Is it too late?" That depends. (Do I sound like a shrink or what?) It depends on a child's age, his personality, how much and how long the culture has intruded, your perseverance in altering course. The ultimate answer is known only to God. In the meantime, you must act as though it's never too late. Change what you believe needs to be changed — discipline, supervision, media freedoms, peer contacts. Insight leads to good change.

"Should I change all at once or focus on one problem at a time?" Change as much as you can as fast as you can. The instant you taste spoiled milk, do you spit it out or do you just sip it more slowly? Turning around a large ship on the ocean can take up to twelve miles. And that's a ship with no kids on board. You're not the size of a ship, but you are far more complex. Altering the course of a ship is child's play compared with altering the course of parenting.

Suppose your initial move is to repeal Freeman's unlimited phone access. As you look back, this is where you've slipped most. Once that's corrected, you'll curb his video game gluttony. But after a month, the phone is still a battle. Do you focus on the phone for another month, while letting the video games play on?

Then, too, how do you measure success? At 100 percent better? 75 percent? 50? Pushing back the culture is a battle that takes place on multiple fronts, with success coming sometimes in little steps, sometimes in leaps. Fifty percent improvement may be major progress, given how long the trouble has been percolating.

Brace yourself: The kids won't welcome this new you. Has some alien invaded your brain? Who have you been talking to? What have you been reading?

How intense might their reaction be? I hope I can't hear it from my house.

Kids don't applaud a parent who abruptly reverses directions—unless it's in their favor, that is. You're changing the rules, now, when everything was just fine as it was. How long before you return to normal? When do they get their freedoms back? Is this just a phase?

Tell your kids that, yes, it is just a phase. But it is one that will last until they're adults. This more self-confident mom or dad is here to stay and will only become more self-confident with time. If little else, your kids will understand when they have kids. Who knows what the culture will look like then.

Winning in the End

The culture is in the air we breathe. There is no way to hold one's breath indefinitely. How deeply you and your children breathe it in, however, remains very much under your control.

Navigating the culture successfully is a demanding journey through the new "enlightened" morality—if one can call it that—propagated by technology, media, and relentless sneaky temptations.

Good parents can feel flummoxed and weary, standing like ever-watchful sentinels over their child's growing up. Nonetheless, they persevere, knowing how high the stakes are.

If, one day, your child turns away from the morals of his upbringing, is all lost? Has all that you've conscientiously taught for so long shown itself to be in vain? And is the "departure" permanent? As always, only God knows for certain. He can see the full stretch of life. We can see only the now, and dimly into the future.

Many young adults, after a foray into the culture's dead ends, look back upon what they knew when younger and get smarter. To quote Mark Twain: "When I was a boy of fourteen, my father was so ignorant I could hardly stand to have the old man around. But when I got to be twenty-one, I was astonished by how much he had learned in seven years."

A grown child may take more than seven years to know how much his parents knew, but one day he may return to understanding and re-embracing their wisdom.

The culture can be relentlessly intrusive. At times its voices may seem too many and too strong to silence. But your voice is strong, too. And you will always have with you the strongest voice of all: prayer.

About the Author

Dr. Ray Guarendi is a Catholic husband and father of ten adopted children, a clinical psychologist, author, professional speaker, and national radio and television host. His radio show, *The Dr. Is In*, can be heard on the EWTN Global Catholic Radio Network on over 350 stations and Sirius XM (channel 130). His TV show, *Living Right with Dr. Ray*, can be seen on EWTN television, reaching more than 340 million homes in 145 countries and territories.